THE HEINZ BARBECUE COOKBOOK

The Heinz BARBECUE COOKBOOK

KEY PORTER BOOKS

National Library of Canada Cataloguing in Publication

Main entry under title:

The Heinz barbecue cookbook.

Includes index.
ISBN 1-55263-459-0

1. Barbecue cookery.

TX840.B3H44 2002   641.5'784   C2002-901628-2

The publisher gratefully acknowledges the support of the Canada Council for the Arts and the Ontario Arts Council for its publishing program.

We acknowledge the financial support of the Government of Canada through the Book Publishing Industry Development Program (BPIDP) for our publishing activities.

Key Porter Books Limited
70 The Esplanade
Toronto, Ontario
Canada M5E 1R2

www.keyporter.com

Design: Peter Maher
Photography: Pete Paterson
Electronic Formatting: Jean Lightfoot Peters
Illustrations: John Lightfoot

Printed and bound in Canada

02 03 04 05 06 07 6 5 4 3 2 1

Acknowledgements

Recipe Development and Writing:

Ted Reader's Chef Developments: Chef Ted Reader
    King of the Q, www.kingoftheq.com
Sous Chef: Mike McColl
Writer/Editor: Craig Thompson

Food and Prop Styling:

Chef Ted Reader
Kester Birch
Shawn Johnson of On the Curve Restaurant,
    Mississauga, Ontario
Chris Powell of On the Curve Restaurant,
    Mississauga, Ontario
Alfredo Venezia
Mike McColl

Contents

Introduction

Heinz was the first company to make ketchup that was free of preservatives. The first bottles of preservative-free ketchup were manufactured in 1906.

Tomatoes are a treasure trove of nutrients including potassium, folic acid, and vitamins A and C.

Welcome to *The Heinz Barbecue Cookbook*! Inside, you'll find a wealth of creative, nutritious, convenient and unbelievably tasty answers to what is perhaps the world's oldest question: "What am I going to make for dinner?"

These days, this question is harder to answer than ever before. If you're like most of the North American population, you're busy! If you're a woman, the situation is particularly tricky. You've got a terrific family, a satisfying career and a bustling social life, but it's still up to you to prepare most of the family meals. Although statistics show that you spend only thirty minutes making dinner (much less than previous generations), you're still concerned about putting a tasty, fun meal on the table—a meal that the whole family or friends will enjoy.

The Heinz Barbecue Cookbook can help. In the pages that follow, you'll find a unique collection of delicious, nutritious, easy-to-prepare recipes for your outdoor or indoor grill. From coast to coast, Canadians are avid grillers. Whether its the product of backyard barbecues on lazy summer days or quick, parka-clad trips to the balcony in the middle of winter, the taste of food fresh off the grill has never been more appealing. In these health-conscious days, grilled food has the added bonus of being good for you. Light marinades replace heavy sauces and a dash of balsamic vinegar is as fine an accompaniment to vegetables as butter. And you can't go wrong by adding tomatoes and processed tomato products to your diet, so full of nutrients and taste.

So where does Heinz fit in? From ketchup, pickles and barbecue sauce to beans, mayonnaise and canned tuna, Heinz products have been embraced by consumers around the world for more than 125 years. The Heinz name carries with it the same tradition of quality and good taste that turned a small family business in Pittsburgh, Pennsylvania, into an on-going international success story.

Heinz's commitment to quality has remained firm throughout the company's history. Back in the early 1900s, founder Henry Heinz was a key part of the battle against mislabeling and false advertising in the food industry—a battle that led to the US Pure Food and Drug Act. Nearly 100 years later, Heinz is still producing foods that stand up to the toughest scrutiny, including condiments that do not contain any preservatives, additives or artificial ingredients.

While the range of products that Heinz produces is impressive, ketchup is by far and away the most popular. If it seems like an everyday ingredient, think again. According to a survey by *Food & Wine Magazine*, chefs at some of New York's finest four-star restaurants admit to using ketchup as a secret ingredient in sauces for everything from cod, to pork, to chicken. Although this "secret weapon" of the cooking world can be found in nearly 75% of North American households and in 140 countries around the world, Canadians consume almost 20% more per capita than their American counterparts—making ketchup a particularly popular ingredient in Canadian kitchens.

Although lycopene is found in some fruits and vegetables, processed tomato products, like ketchup, contain much more.

Along with a host of other Heinz products, ketchup will be a key ingredient in the recipes found on the pages that follow. Taking a cue from those master chefs in New York, the Heinz test kitchen has compiled a collection of wholesome and delicious taste sensations that start with basic ingredients. Try Heinz 57 Tomato Gazpacho on a hot summer day, or BBQ Coleslaw for the next family get-together. Fire-Roasted

Ketchup was first invented in China more than 300 years ago. It was originally made from spiced fish, not tomatoes, and was called "ketsiap." The British brought the condiment to Europe in the 18th century, where they adapted the recipe to suit their tastes by making it with tomatoes.

New independent studies by the University of Toronto have concluded that consuming processed tomato products, like ketchup, may help significantly raise levels of lycopene in the human body.

Heinz ketchups have been sold around the world almost since the company began. However, different countries prefer different tastes in their ketchups: Western Europeans like their ketchup spicy, while Canadians, Australians, and Venezuelans prefer their ketchup to be sweet.

Chili Bruschetta and BBQ Chicken Wings are great for before the big game, while Roasted Garlic Lamb Chops are fit for any dinner party. Chicken lovers will dive right into Grilled Mango Chicken, while those that prefer seafood will want to try Hot and Spicy Grilled Shrimp. And everyone will love the Classic Canadian Burger. Recipes for terrific side dishes and spectacular desserts will help you complete your meal. Each of these fabulous dishes uses one or more Heinz products as its base, proving that when you trust your ingredients, you can dare to be a little different.

In addition to being appetizing and good for you, the recipes in this book were all designed to fit into your busy schedule—each can be prepared in under 30 minutes. So fire up the grill, gather your family and friends, and get ready to cook up a storm. You'll be amazed by the results.

Seasoning
Heinz 57 Barbecue Seasoning Rub

Throughout this book reference is made to Heinz 57 Barbecue Seasoning Rub. This barbecue seasoning is a simple recipe that features a blend of a variety of commonly available spices. You can make the blend yourself using fresh spices—but be sure to store the seasoning in an airtight container away from heat and light. That way it should last a few months.

Of course, if you're not up to the challenge or don't have the time to make the blend yourself you can always buy a store-bought seasoning. This homemade method is only a suggestion; you can adapt the recipe to suit your personal taste.

This seasoning is great when rubbed onto chicken, ribs, seafood and steaks.

Makes approximately 2½ cups (600 ml)

½ cup	125 ml	Hungarian paprika
¼ cup	50 ml	kosher salt
¼ cup	50 ml	chili powder
3 tbsp	45 ml	granulated sugar
2 tbsp	25 ml	cayenne pepper
2 tbsp	25 ml	ground cumin
2 tbsp	25 ml	mustard powder
2 tbsp	25 ml	garlic powder
2 tbsp	25 ml	granulated onion
1 tbsp	15 ml	dried thyme
1 tbsp	15 ml	dried basil
1 tbsp	15 ml	dried oregano
1 tbsp	15 ml	coarse ground black pepper
1 tbsp	15 ml	ground coriander

1. Mix together the paprika, salt, chili powder, sugar, cayenne, cumin, mustard, garlic, onion, thyme, basil, oregano, black pepper and coriander.
2. Store in an airtight container in a cool, dry place away from light and heat.
3. Use by rubbing the spices all over the meat or seafood, pressing the seasoning into the food.

Summer Soups

Heinz 57 Tomato Gazpacho

Heinz Chili Sauce Ice Cubes

Grilled Chicken, Corn, and Sausage Chowder

Heinz 57 Tomato Gazpacho

Gazpacho is a wonderful chilled soup for those hot summer days when you are hungry but too hot to eat. Serve in chilled soup bowls garnished with Heinz Chili Sauce ice cubes (see page 16).

Serves 8
Preparation time:
  30 minutes
Chilling time: 1 hour

6 ripe		plum tomatoes, diced
1 small		red onion, diced
1		jalapeno pepper, seeded and chopped
2 cloves		garlic, finely chopped
1 medium		English cucumber, peeled, seeded, and chopped
1 bottle	455 ml	Heinz Chili Sauce, Chunky with Sweet Peppers
2 cups	500 ml	Heinz Tomato Juice
1		lime, juiced
1 tbsp	15 ml	chopped fresh dill
2 tsp	10 ml	Heinz Worcestershire Sauce
¼ cup	50 ml	olive oil
		salt and freshly ground pepper
8		dill sprigs
		French baguette, sliced

1. In a food processor or blender combine the tomatoes, onion, jalapeno, garlic, and cucumber. Pulse for 1–2 minutes. Add the Heinz Chili Sauce and tomato juice and blend until smooth.
2. Add lime juice, dill, Worcestershire sauce and olive oil. Season to taste with salt and pepper and pulse again.
3. Pour into a glass serving bowl and chill for 1 hour.
4. To serve, ladle the gazpacho into soup bowls and garnish with Heinz Chili Sauce Ice Cubes and a sprig of fresh dill. Serve with fresh baguette.

Dillweed
- Dillweed has a delicate flavour
- Used for pickling and in vegetable dips
- Delicious in potato, cucumber, and carrot dishes and great on fresh or smoked fish and seafood
- Used in ancient times to lull babies to sleep

Remember: Use flavouring to enhance, not overwhelm, other flavours in the dish.

Heinz Chili Sauce Ice Cubes

Makes 12–16 ice cubes

First grown in the Andes Mountains in South America, tomatoes are now grown in virtually every country in the world and have revolutionized diets everywhere.

This is a technique that many top restaurants use. The ice cube performs several functions: it keeps the soup nicely chilled; turns everyday gazpacho into something extraordinary; adds a distinct flavour when it melts; and will have your guests raving.

1 cup	250 ml	Heinz Chili Sauce, Chunky with Sweet Peppers
1 cup	250 ml	Heinz Tomato Juice
¼ cup	50 ml	cold water

1. In a bowl combine the Heinz Chili Sauce, tomato juice, and water. Pour mixture into ice cube tray and freeze until solid.

Grilled Chicken, Corn, and Sausage Chowder

The flavours of grilled chicken and lightly charred corn make this soup a winner for summer evenings. Chunky sweet pepper chili sauce creates a colourful garnish for this chowder.

Serves 8–10
Marinade time: 2–4 hours
Grilling time: 20 minutes
Cooking time: 1 hour

2 x 6 oz	165 g	chicken breasts, boneless and skinless
¾ cup	180 ml	Diana's Marinade, Garlic and Herbs
4 ears		peaches and cream corn on the cob, shucked salt and freshly ground pepper
3 tbsp	45 ml	vegetable oil
1 large		Spanish onion, quartered
2 x 3 oz	75 g	smoked sausages
3 tbsp	45 ml	butter
4 cloves		garlic, finely chopped
2 cups	500 ml	Yukon gold potatoes, peeled and cut into ½ inch (1 cm) cubes
3 tbsp	45 ml	Heinz 57 BBQ Seasoning Rub (see page 11)
6 cups	1.5 l	chicken stock
2 tbsp	25 ml	chopped fresh oregano
1 cup	250 ml	whipping cream
1 tbsp	15 ml	Heinz Worcestershire Sauce fresh sprigs of oregano
8–10 tbsp	120–150 ml	Heinz Chili Sauce Chunky with Sweet Peppers

Sage
- A fragrant aroma and an astringent but warm flavour
- One of the most commonly used herbs in the world
- Sage enhances pork, lamb, meats, and sausages
- Ancient Greeks and Romans used sage to cure snakebites and to invigorate the mind and body
- In the Middle Ages, people used sage to treat colds, fevers, liver trouble, and epilepsy

Remember: If using fresh sage, chop leaves for fullest flavour.

1. Place the chicken breasts in a glass dish and pour the Diana's Marinade over, turning to evenly coat. Cover and refrigerate for 2–4 hours.
2. Preheat grill to medium-high.
3. Rub the cobs of corn and onions with vegetable oil and season with salt and pepper.

4. Remove chicken breasts from Diana's Marinade, discarding marinade, and grill for 5–6 minutes per side, until fully cooked.
5. Grill corn and onions for 5–8 minutes until slightly charred and golden brown.
6. Grill smoked sausages for 8–10 minutes until slightly charred and golden brown.
7. Remove chicken, corn, onions, and sausages from grill and allow to cool.
8. Cut the chicken and sausages into 1 inch (2.5 cm) cubes.
9. Using a sharp knife, cut the grilled corn kernels from the cob and dice the onion.
10. In a large soup pot melt the butter over medium heat. Add the garlic and grilled onion; cook for 3–4 minutes or until tender. Add the potatoes and cook for another 3–4 minutes.
11. Add the Heinz 57 BBQ Seasoning Rub and chicken stock. Bring to a boil, reduce heat, and simmer the soup uncovered, stirring occasionally, for 45 minutes or until the potatoes are soft and the soup is thickened. If necessary, add a little more stock to thin the soup.
12. Add the grilled corn kernels, chicken, sausage, oregano, and cream, and simmer another 15 minutes.
13. Season soup to taste with Worcestershire sauce, salt, and pepper.
14. When serving the chowder, garnish each bowl with a fresh sprig of oregano and a large dollop of Heinz Chili Sauce Chunky with Sweet Peppers.

Garden-Fresh Salads

Grilled Vegetable Salad with Goat's Cheese and
   Tangy Tomato Dressing

Tangy Tomato Salad Dressing

Grilled Potato Salad with Kickers Barbecue
   Dressing

Rainbow Bean Salad

Tuscan Grilled Chicken Salad

Basil and Oregano Kickers Shrimp in Penne
   Pasta Salad

Tomato, Onion, Fennel, and Bocconcini Salad

BBQ Coleslaw

Grilled Vegetable Salad with Goat's Cheese and Tangy Tomato Dressing

There is nothing like the flavor of grilled summer vegetables. Add a bit of red onion, peppers, and some goat's cheese, and you've got a summer salad that really sparkles.

Serves 8
Preparation time:
  15 minutes
Grill time: 20 minutes

1 large		red onion, sliced into ½ inch (1 cm) slices
2		zucchini, thinly sliced diagonally
8 large		field mushrooms, quartered
1		red or yellow pepper, sliced into 1 inch (2.5 cm) rounds
1 bunch		asparagus, cut into 3 inch (7.5 cm) lengths
1 tbsp	15 ml	Heinz 57 BBQ Seasoning Rub (see page 11)
2 tbsp	25 ml	olive oil
2 tbsp	25 ml	Heinz Red Wine Flavoured Vinegar
½–¾ cup	125–180 ml	Tangy Tomato Salad Dressing (see page 22)
½ cup	125 ml	crumbled goat's cheese
1 tbsp	15 ml	chopped fresh cilantro
		salt and freshly ground pepper

Contrary to popular belief, acidity levels don't differ between types of tomatoes. Those that taste "less acidic" simply possess more natural sugars.

1. Preheat grill to medium-high.
2. In a large bowl toss the red onion, zucchini, mushrooms, pepper, and asparagus together.
3. Add barbecue seasoning, olive oil, and vinegar and mix thoroughly. Place mixture in a grilling basket.
4. Grill vegetables for 8–10 minutes per side until lightly charred and tender.
5. Remove vegetables from the basket and place in a large bowl. Toss with dressing, crumbled goat's cheese, and chopped fresh cilantro.
6. Season to taste with salt and pepper.

Tangy Tomato Salad Dressing

Makes about 2½ cups (600 ml)

Preparation time: 10 minutes

An ideal dressing for any salad, this recipe is made easy by using Heinz Ketchup and Heinz Chili Sauce—two pre-pared ingredients that make this a quick dressing with a distinct taste.

¾ cup	180 ml	Heinz Tomato Ketchup
½ cup	125 ml	Heinz Chili Sauce
½ cup	125 ml	Heinz Red Wine Flavoured Vinegar
¼ cup	50 ml	vegetable oil
¼ cup	50 ml	water
1 tbsp	15 ml	Heinz Worcestershire Sauce
1 tbsp	15 ml	granulated sugar
2		green onions, finely chopped
2 cloves		garlic, minced
1 tbsp	15 ml	dill
1 tsp	5 ml	cayenne pepper
1 tsp	5 ml	coarse freshly ground black pepper
		salt to taste

1. Combine Heinz Ketchup, Heinz Chili Sauce, vinegar, oil, water, Worcestershire sauce, sugar, green onions, garlic, dill, cayenne, and pepper in a mixing bowl and whisk together until fully blended.
2. Transfer to a covered container and refrigerate for at least 1 hour. Season to taste with salt. Toss with fresh lettuce salads, tomato salads, and grilled vegetables.

Cayenne Pepper

- Little aroma but extremely hot
- Heats up stir-fries, curries, meatloaf, savoury biscuits, marinades, sweet potatoes, corn, pork, steak, poultry, and shellfish
- Commonly used in Mexican and Italian cooking
- Spanish explorers reported that Native Americans ate this pepper-like fruit "like we eat apples"

Remember: Keep refrigerated.

Grilled Potato Salad
with Kickers Barbecue Dressing

When grilling vegetables on the barbecue we recommend that you use a specially designed grilling basket, which can be found in most hardware stores. A grilling basket allows you to turn all the vegetables at once, resulting in a more even and faster cooking. And vegetables don't fall through the grill!

2 lbs	900 g	mini white new potatoes
1 small		red onion, sliced into ½ inch (1 cm) slices
2 medium		leeks, sliced in half lengthways, washed and cut into 1 inch (2.5 cm) pieces
1 medium		red pepper, cut into 1 inch (2.5 cm) strips
3 cloves		garlic, minced
1 tbsp	15 ml	Heinz 57 BBQ Seasoning Rub (see page 11)
3 tbsp	45 ml	vegetable oil
2 tbsp	25 ml	chopped fresh parsley
1 cup	250 ml	cubed yellow cheddar cheese salt and freshly ground pepper

Serves 8
Preparation time:
  30 minutes
Grill time: 15 minutes

Kickers Barbecue Dressing
makes approximately
  2 cups (500 ml)
Preparation time:
  10 minutes

STARTING UP
Always start the grill with the lid up to ensure proper ventilation. Once the flame ignites, close the lid and preheat to the desired temperature.

1. In a large pot, boil the potatoes in salted water for 15–20 minutes until just tender.
2. Drain and cool.
3. Cut the new potatoes into halves or quarters, so they are uniform in size.
4. In a large bowl combine the cooked potatoes, red onion, leeks, red pepper, garlic, barbecue seasoning, and vegetable oil. Mix thoroughly.
5. Preheat grill to medium-high.
6. Place potato mixture in a grilling basket and grill for 12–15 minutes, turning the basket twice, until lightly charred and tender. Transfer vegetables to a large mixing bowl.

7. Add the barbecue dressing (see recipe below), parsley, and cheddar cheese. Season to taste with salt and pepper and serve immediately.

Kickers Barbecue Dressing

3 cloves		garlic, minced
2 tbsp	25 ml	prepared horseradish
2 tsp	10 ml	Heinz 57 BBQ Seasoning Rub (see page 11)
½ cup	125 ml	Heinz Tomato Juice
½ cup	125 ml	Heinz Ketchup Kickers, Sweet Basil and Oregano
2 tbsp	25 ml	Heinz Pure Apple Cider Vinegar
½ cup	125 ml	olive oil
1 tsp	15 ml	Heinz Worcestershire Sauce
		salt and freshly ground pepper

1. In a glass bowl combine the garlic, horseradish, barbecue seasoning, tomato juice, Heinz Ketchup Kickers, and apple cider vinegar.
2. Slowly add the olive oil in a steady stream while continuously whisking to emulsify the dressing. Season to taste with Worcestershire sauce, salt, and pepper.
3. Transfer to a covered container and refrigerate for at least 1 hour.

Rainbow Bean Salad

Bean salad is a tradition at most summer picnics, and this quick recipe provides a rainbow of colours and flavours—a combination of fresh yellow and green beans with a blend of Heinz Kidney Beans and BBQ Style Beans.

Serves 8
Preparation time:
   20 minutes

2 cups	500 g	fresh green beans
2 cups	500 g	fresh yellow wax beans
1 can (14 oz)	398 ml	Heinz Red Kidney Beans, drained
1 can (14 oz)	398 ml	Heinz BBQ Style White and Red Kidney Beans, drained
1 medium		red onion, thinly sliced
1 of each		green, red, and yellow peppers, thinly sliced
3		green onions, chopped
1 cup	250 ml	Heinz Chili Sauce, Chunky with Sweet Peppers
2 tbsp	25 ml	Heinz Pure Apple Cider Vinegar
2 tbsp	25 ml	chopped fresh parsley
		salt and freshly ground pepper

1. Trim the ends of the green and yellow beans.
2. Bring a pot of water to a rolling boil and cook the green and yellow beans for 1–2 minutes. Drain and cool under cold running water. Drain again.
3. In a large bowl combine the blanched beans, kidney beans, Heinz BBQ Style beans, red onion, peppers, green onions, Heinz Chili Sauce, vinegar, and parsley. Season to taste with salt and pepper and mix thoroughly.
4. Chill for 1 hour and serve.

Tuscan Grilled Chicken Salad

Imagine a summer picnic in the hills of Tuscany and you've captured the inspiration behind Tuscan Grilled Chicken Salad—a cool dish on a hot day. The chicken breasts are marinated, grilled, then chilled and tossed with seasonal vegetables to make this salad healthy and appetizing.

Serves 8
Marinade time: 2–4 hours
Grill time: 20 minutes
Preparation time:
  30 minutes

4 x 6 oz	165 g	boneless skinless chicken breasts
1 cup	250 ml	Diana's Marinade, Lemon and Pepper
2 cups	500 g	halved ripe cherry tomatoes
1 medium		green pepper, cubed
1 medium		sweet yellow onion, sliced
1 small		English cucumber, peeled and cut into 1 inch (2.5 cm) chunks
½ cup	125 g	black olives
1 cup	250 ml	cubed feta cheese
1 tbsp	15 ml	chopped fresh basil
¼ cup	50 ml	Heinz Pure Malt Vinegar
¼ cup	50 ml	olive oil
		salt and freshly ground pepper

1. Place the chicken breasts in a glass dish and pour in the Diana's Marinade, turning to coat evenly. Cover and refrigerate for 2–4 hours.
2. Preheat grill to medium-high.
3. Remove chicken breasts from Diana's Marinade, discarding marinade, and grill for 5–6 minutes per side, until fully cooked.
4. Let chicken cool completely before slicing into 1 inch (2.5 cm) pieces.
5. In a large bowl combine the tomatoes, pepper, onion, cucumber, olives, feta cheese, basil, and grilled chicken. Add vinegar and oil and season to taste with salt and pepper. Toss gently to thoroughly mix.
6. Cover and chill for 1 hour before serving.

TOOLS OF THE TRADE
Regular kitchen utensils don't often stand up to the rough-and-tumble world of grilling. Always buy specialty barbecue accessories for convenience and comfort.

Basil and Oregano Kickers Shrimp in Penne Pasta Salad

Serves 8
Preparation time:
  30 minutes

If you have a weakness for shrimp and love it when it's mixed with your favourite pasta, then you'll enjoy this simple salad. It's a salad with tomato character touched off with the wonderful taste of sun-dried tomatoes.

THE JOY OF GRILLING
With grilling, location is everything. Position your barbecue away from trees, at least 10 feet from the nearest building, away from motor vehicles, and out of the wind.

1 lb	454 g	dried penne
2 tbsp	25 ml	olive oil
1 cup	250 ml	thinly sliced sun-dried tomatoes
2 stalks		celery, thinly sliced diagonally
4		green onions, chopped
1		sweet yellow onion, sliced
2 tbsp	25 g	chopped fresh flat leaf parsley
2 cups	500 ml	frozen baby shrimp, thawed and drained
¾ cup	180 ml	mayonnaise
¼ cup	50 ml	Heinz Ketchup Kickers, Sweet Basil and Oregano
¼ cup	50 ml	Heinz Chili Sauce, Chunky with Sweet Peppers
1–2 tbsp	15–25 ml	fresh squeezed lemon juice
		salt and freshly ground pepper

1. Cook pasta as per package instructions. Drain pasta and run cold water over it for several minutes. Place drained pasta in a bowl and toss with olive oil. Spread hot pasta on a baking sheet and allow to cool completely. Transfer cooled pasta to a large bowl.
2. Add sun-dried tomatoes, celery, green and yellow onion, parsley, and shrimp and toss.
3. In a small bowl whisk together the mayonnaise, Heinz Ketchup Kickers, Heinz Chili Sauce, and lemon juice. Add dressing to the pasta mixture and thoroughly mix.
4. Adjust seasoning with salt and pepper.

Tomato, Onion, Fennel, and Bocconcini Salad

The inspiration for this salad comes from the hills of Italy where ripe tomatoes and bocconcini (baby mozzarella) are served al fresco in the cobblestone streets of villages. We've added a few extra touches to this traditional salad to give it more substance.

Serves 8
Preparation time:
 30 minutes

12 ripe		plum tomatoes
8		bocconcini, quartered
1 medium		red onion, thinly sliced
1 head		fennel, thinly sliced
4		green onions, finely chopped
2 tbsp	25 ml	chopped fresh basil
1 tbsp	15 ml	Heinz Worcestershire Sauce
¼ cup	50 ml	Heinz Chili Sauce
¼ cup	50 ml	Heinz Red Wine Flavoured Vinegar
¼ cup	50 ml	olive oil
		salt and freshly ground black pepper

Tomatoes come in a variety of colours including white, purple, green, yellow, and orange. Unfortunately, only red tomatoes possess the beneficial antioxidant lycopene. The redder the tomato, the higher the levels of lycopene.

1. Slice the tomatoes in half lengthwise, and then cut each half into 4 or 6 wedges.
2. In a large bowl mix together the tomato wedges, bocconcini, red onion, fennel, green onion, and basil and set aside.
3. In a small bowl whisk together the Worcestershire sauce, Heinz Chili Sauce, vinegar, and olive oil.
4. Pour dressing over tomato salad, tossing to mix thoroughly. Season to taste with salt and pepper.
5. Serve immediately.

BBQ Coleslaw

Serves 8
Perparation time:
15–20 minutes

CLEANING A WOODEN
CUTTING BOARD
Always clean a wooden cutting
board by hand, not in the dish-
washer. Scrub it with hot soapy
water, then use a lemon half to
rub salt into the wood, and rinse.
Pat dry with a towel and let
stand to dry so the wood won't
warp or split.

Grilled ribs and chicken wouldn't be complete without coleslaw. This funky recipe uses Heinz Ketchup Kickers Hot and Spicy for the dressing.

½ head		green cabbage, sliced very fine
1 medium		onion, finely chopped
2 large		carrots, grated
3		green onions
2		jalapeno peppers, seeded and finely diced
1 tbsp	15 ml	sugar
2 tbsp	25 ml	Heinz Pure White Vinegar
½ cup	125 ml	Heinz Ketchup Kickers, Hot and Spicy
½ cup	125 ml	vegetable oil
1 tbsp	15 ml	Heinz 57 BBQ Seasoning Rub (see page 11)

1. In a large bowl mix the cabbage, onion, carrots, green onions, and jalapeno peppers. Set aside.
2. In a small bowl whisk together the sugar, vinegar, Heinz Ketchup Kickers, oil, and barbecue seasoning.
3. Pour dressing over the cabbage mixture. Toss to mix and let stand for 1–2 hours, tossing occasionally.
4. Refrigerate until ready to serve.

Appetizers and Snacks

Fire-Roasted Chili Bruschetta

Oriental Chicken Satay

BBQ Chicken Wings—Two Flavours

Knife and Fork Grilled Chicken and Cheese
   Quesadillas

BBQ Steak Nachos

Grilled Butterflied Jumbo Shrimp

Grilled Vegetable-Stuffed Portobello
   Mushrooms

Fire-Roasted Chili Bruschetta

For a change, try making bruschetta on the grill. The smoke will bring out the flavours of the tomatoes, onions, garlic, and olives to give you an appetizer that will dance its way across your palette.

Serves 6–8
Preparation time:
  30 minutes
Grilling time: 15 minutes

8–10		plum tomatoes, cut in half lengthwise
1 large		onion, cut in ½-inch (1 cm) rounds
½ cup	125 ml	olive oil
2 tbsp	25 ml	Heinz 57 BBQ Seasoning Rub (see page 11)
1 cup	250 ml	Heinz Chili Sauce
½ cup	125 ml	Heinz Ketchup Kickers, Sweet Basil and Oregano
4 cloves		garlic, minced
1		baguette
½ cup	125 ml	parmesan cheese, grated
		salt and pepper

When tomatoes first arrived in Europe from North America, people believed they had special powers that could make people fall in love. That's why tomatoes are still known in some circles as "love apples."

1. Preheat grill to medium-high.
2. Toss the tomatoes and onions in half the olive oil and barbecue seasoning and grill for 10–12 minutes or until charred and softened (the onions may take a little longer than the tomatoes). Turn once or twice for even grilling.
3. Allow the tomatoes and onions to cool to room temperature and chop coarsely.
4. Toss the tomato and onions, Heinz Chili Sauce, Heinz Ketchup Kickers, garlic, and the remaining olive oil and season to taste with salt and pepper. Let sit for a half-hour at room temperature.
5. Slice the baguette on an angle into 10–12 thick slices and toast both sides lightly on the grill, spacing them evenly on a grill tray.
6. Divide the chili bruschetta mix evenly over the slices of toasted bread and top with parmesan.
7. Place the tray on the grill and close the lid. After 5 minutes this delicious bruschetta is ready to eat.

Oriental Chicken Satay

Chicken satay is a delightful addition to any appetizer tray. The bite-sized morsels of chicken succulent with ginger, sesame oil, and honey garlic barbecue sauce will melt in your mouth.

Serves 8
Marinade time: 1 hour
Preparation time:
  25 minutes
Grilling time: 10 minutes

4–6 x 6 oz each	165 g each	chicken breasts, boneless and skinless
1 cup	250 ml	Diana's Marinade, Teriyaki
1 cup	250 ml	Diana Sauce, Honey Garlic
¼ cup	50 ml	soy sauce
2 tbsp	25 ml	ginger, minced
2 tsp	10 ml	sesame oil
1 tsp	5 ml	hot pepper sauce

1. Soak 24 wooden skewers in lukewarm water for at least 15 minutes.
2. Slice each chicken breast into 4 long thin strips and marinate in Diana's Teriyaki Marinade for 2 hours, refrigerated.
3. For the glaze, mix together the barbecue sauce, soy sauce, ginger, sesame oil, and hot pepper sauce.
4. Thread the chicken strips onto the soaked skewers and discard any marinade.
5. Preheat grill to medium-high.
6. Place the chicken on the grill with the ends of the skewers hanging off the edge of the hot cooking surface. Grill for about 3–5 minutes per side or until fully cooked.
7. Brush liberally with glaze while cooking.
8. Serve immediately.

Ginger
- Hot taste with woody, sweet aroma
- Perks up fruit, lemon, and chocolate desserts
- Great for seasoning stir-fries, curries, duck, glazed ham, and seafood
- Use in muffins, crisps, cookies, tea, and lemonade

Remember: Give herbs and spices the "nose test" occasionally. If fragrance is no longer strong, replace with fresh supplies.

BBQ Chicken Wings—Two Flavours

These are finger-licking, lip-smacking chicken wings—like the ones you find in your favourite bar but done exactly the way you like them. At home you can choose the sauce you like best. Here are two recipes—one for honey garlic sauce, the other for Buffalo-style barbecue sauce.

3 lb	1.5 kg	jumbo chicken wings
3 tbsp	45 ml	Diana's Marinade, Lemon and Pepper
3 tbsp	45 ml	vegetable oil

Honey Garlic Sauce

1 cup	250 ml	Heinz Western Grill Honey Garlic BBQ Sauce
¼ cup	50 ml	honey
1 tbsp	15 ml	cracked black pepper
1 tbsp	15 ml	Heinz Worcestershire Sauce

Buffalo-Style Sauce

½ cup	125 ml	Heinz Ketchup Kickers, Hot and Spicy
½ cup	125 ml	Heinz Western Grill Original BBQ Sauce
2 tbsp	25 ml	hot sauce
¼ cup	50 ml	butter, melted

Serves 6–8
Marinade time: 2–4 hours
Preparation time:
   20 minutes
Grilling time:
   20–30 minutes

A CLEAN GRILL IS A SAFE GRILL Grease buildup on the grill can lead to flare-ups. Always clean your grill before and after use with a stiff wire brush. A light coating of cooking oil applied to the grill before lighting will prevent food from sticking and make the grill easier to clean.

1. Trim wing tips from wings and cut through the joint to separate the winglet from the drummette. Place wing pieces in a large bowl and toss with Diana's Lemon and Pepper Marinade and vegetable oil. Cover and refrigerate for 2 to 4 hours.
2. For the honey garlic wings, combine barbecue sauce, honey, black pepper, and Worcestershire sauce and set aside.
3. For the Buffalo-style sauce, combine Heinz Ketchup Kickers, Heinz Barbecue Sauce, hot sauce, and butter and set aside.
4. Preheat grill to medium.

5. Remove wings from Diana's Marinade, discarding marinade.
6. Place seasoned wings on the grill for 10–12 minutes per side, turning every 5–6 minutes or until fully cooked, golden, and crisp.
7. Remove wings from the grill and divide the wings between two bowls. Add the Buffalo sauce to one bowl and the honey garlic to the other bowl and toss.
8. Serve with celery and carrot sticks and blue cheese dip.

Knife and Fork Grilled Chicken and Cheese Quesadillas

Most quesadillas qualify as finger food, but this recipe is so chock-full of stuffing that you will have to use a knife and fork to catch everything.

Serves 8
Marinade time: 2–4 hours
Preparation time:
  30 minutes
Grilling time: 20 minutes

2		chicken breasts, boneless and skinless
1 cup	250 ml	Diana's Marinade, Lemon and Pepper
3		green onions, chopped
½ cup	125 ml	Heinz Chili Sauce, Chunky with Sweet Pepper
1 cup	250 ml	cheddar cheese, grated
1 cup	250 ml	monterey jack cheese, grated
4 large		tortillas
1 cup	250 ml	Heinz Western Grill Original BBQ Sauce
1 cup	250 ml	sour cream

1. Place chicken in a glass dish and pour Diana's Marinade over, turning once to coat evenly. Cover and refrigerate for 2–4 hours.
2. Preheat grill to medium-high.
3. Remove chicken from Diana's Marinade, discarding marinade. Grill 5–6 minutes per side, or until fully cooked.
4. During grilling, brush chicken with half of the Heinz Barbecue Sauce.
5. Remove chicken from grill and allow to cool, then slice thinly.
6. Mix the chicken strips, green onions, Heinz Chili Sauce, cheddar, and monterey jack. Place one-quarter of the mixture in the centre of each tortilla. Fold the tortilla in half, keeping the filling inside.
7. Preheat grill to medium. Grill the quesadillas for 2–3 minutes on each side until crisp and the chicken and cheese mixture is hot.
8. Brush both sides with Heinz Barbecue Sauce and grill for 1–2 minutes more on each side.
9. Garnish with sour cream. Serve with a knife and fork.

STUCK ON YOU

Food sticking is a common problem—especially with chicken and fish. To avoid sticking, make sure the grill is cleaned and oiled before lighting. Then preheat the grill for a few minutes before cooking.

BBQ Steak Nachos

Serves 4

Preparation time:
30–45 minutes

Grilling time: 15 minutes

Create a Mexican Aztec pyramid with this delicious nacho recipe that uses sirloin steak. It's fun to make and the result is an extraordinary nacho presentation.

1 lb	454 g	sirloin steak
2 tbsp	25 ml	Heinz 57 BBQ Seasoning Rub (see page 11)
1 cup	250 ml	Heinz Western Grill BBQ Sauce
1 tbsp	15 ml	Heinz Worcestershire Sauce
2 tbsp	25 ml	Heinz Pure Apple Cider Vinegar
1 tbsp	15 ml	brown sugar
4 cloves		garlic, minced
1 bag		nacho corn chips
2 cups	500 ml	cheddar cheese, grated
1 medium		green pepper, finely diced
1 small		onion, finely diced
3		tomatoes, finely diced
1 cup	250 ml	Heinz Chili Sauce
1 can (14 oz)	398 ml	Heinz Chili-Style Pinto and Red Kidney Beans
2		green onions, finely chopped

1. Rub the sirloin steak with Heinz 57 BBQ Seasoning Rub, pressing the mixture into the meat.
2. Preheat grill to medium-high
3. For the mesquite sauce, combine barbecue sauce, Worcestershire sauce, vinegar, brown sugar, and garlic in a small sauce pot and bring to a boil; reduce heat and simmer for 10 minutes. Set aside.
4. Place the sirloin steak on the grill and cook for 2–3 minutes per side or until medium-rare. Brush with mesquite sauce. Remove steak from the grill and let stand for a few minutes before slicing thinly.

5. On a large ovenproof tray, layer the nachos with the cheese, pepper, onion, tomatoes, chili sauce, beans, and the steak, creating a small pyramid.
6. Place on grill for about 5 minutes, or until all the cheese is melted.
7. Garnish with green onions.
8. Serve with sour cream and salsa.

LOW ON GAS

Avoid the embarrassment of running out of fuel halfway through your grilling time! Here are a few tips to check your gas level.

- *Purchase a gas gauge at a hardware store.*
- *Check the tank by lifting it; a full tank will weigh about 40 pounds.*
- *Check by feeling the tank. The full portion of the tank will feel slightly chilled.*

Grilled Butterflied Jumbo Shrimp

Shrimp make a delicious appetizer, and you can prepare this dish and serve it in under an hour. Butterflying the shrimp exposes more of the meat, allowing the marinade to be absorbed.

Serves 4
Marinade time: 15 minutes
Preparation time:
  30 minutes
Grilling time: 5–10 minutes

2 lb	900 g	jumbo shrimp
1 cup	250 ml	Diana's Marinade, Garlic and Herbs
¼ cup	50 ml	Heinz Chili Sauce
¼ cup	50 ml	orange juice
½ cup	125 ml	Diana Sauce, Fine Herbs with Lemon
2 tbsp	25 ml	garlic, minced
1 bunch		chives, finely chopped
1 tbsp	15 ml	Heinz 57 BBQ Seasoning Rub (see page 11)
2 oz	60 ml	rum

DULL AND DANGEROUS
A dull knife is a dangerous knife because it requires more force to cut and thus is more likely to slip.

1. Peel and devein shrimp. Place the shrimp on a cutting board and, with a small sharp knife, slice the shrimp down the back, leaving the two sides attached at the tail.
2. Marinate shrimp for 15 minutes in Diana's Garlic and Herbs Marinade.
3. Preheat grill to medium-high.
4. In a small bowl combine the chili sauce, orange juice, Diana Sauce, garlic, chives, barbecue seasoning, and rum.
5. Remove the shrimp from the marinade, discarding marinade, and grill for 3 to 5 minutes per side, brushing with orange-chili barbecue sauce.
6. Serve immediately.

Grilled Vegetable-Stuffed Portobello Mushrooms

Portobello mushrooms are as delicious and meaty as steak when cooked on the grill. They also make excellent appetizers. This recipe uses the mushroom as the centrepiece of a stuffing mixture that features a variety of vegetables with a sweet pepper and bacon serenade.

Serves 6
Preparation: 30 minutes
Grilling time: 30 minutes

6 large		portobello mushrooms, stemmed
¼ cup	50 ml	olive oil
¼ cup	50 ml	Heinz Pure Malt Vinegar
2 tbsp	25 ml	Heinz 57 BBQ Seasoning Rub (see page 11)
1 medium		red pepper, seeded, stemmed, and sliced
1 medium		zucchini, sliced lengthwise in three
1 large		onion, peeled and sliced in ¼-inch (0.5 cm) rounds
8 slices		bacon, diced and fried until crisp
2 cups	500 ml	grated mozzarella cheese
¼ cup	50 ml	Heinz Ketchup Kickers, Roasted Garlic
¼ cup	50 ml	Heinz Chili Sauce, Chunky with Sweet Peppers
¼ cup	50 ml	breadcrumbs
2 tbsp	25 ml	garlic, minced

How Hot Is Hot?
Here's a quick temperature guide.
- *550° is for searing steaks and chops—too hot for cooking.*
- *450° is medium-high heat—perfect for hamburgers and veggies.*
- *350° is low heat and works best for rotisserie cooking, grilling fish, roasting, and for very lean food. Most cooking can be done on low.*

1. Soak portobello mushrooms in warm water for 10 minutes. Remove mushrooms from water and drain on paper towels.
2. In a bowl combine the oil, Heinz vinegar, and barbecue seasoning. Place mushrooms in a glass dish, gill side up. Pour half of the oil and vinegar mixture into the gills of the mushrooms and marinate for 15 minutes.
3. Preheat grill to medium-high.
4. Grill mushrooms for 4 to 5 minutes per side until lightly charred and just tender. Remove from grill and allow to cool.

5. Toss the pepper, zucchini, and onion with the remaining oil, vinegar and barbecue seasoning mixture. Place in a grill basket and grill for 8–12 minutes per side or until lightly charred and tender. Carefully remove the vegetables from the grilling basket and allow to cool.
6. Chop the vegetables and add the bacon, cheese, Heinz Ketchup Kickers, Heinz Chili Sauce, breadcrumbs, and garlic and mix.
7. Divide the stuffing mixture equally between the grilled portobello mushroom caps.
8. Place stuffed portobellos on preheated medium grill and cook for 8–10 minutes until heated through and the cheese melts.

Grilled Sandwiches

Grilled Salmon Sandwich with Green Apple
   Slaw

Truck Stop Steak Sandwich

Sausage and Peppers Sandwich

Grilled Chicken Clubhouse with Canadian
   Bacon

Chili Cheese Dogs

Great Canadian Chicken Burger

Great Canadian Bacon Cheeseburger

Grilled Salmon Sandwich with Green Apple Slaw

This recipe uses the grill to take salmon sandwiches to new heights. Tender, flaky grilled salmon combines with the tangy sweetness of Granny Smith apples to make this a refreshing summer lunch.

Serves 4
Makes 4 sandwiches
Preparation time:
  20 minutes
Grilling time: 15 minutes

4 x 4 oz	110 g	boneless, skinless Atlantic salmon fillets
2 tbsp	25 ml	Heinz 57 BBQ Seasoning Rub (see page 11)
2 tbsp	25 ml	vegetable oil
2		Granny Smith apples, thinly sliced
1 small		red onion, thinly sliced
1 tbsp	15 ml	lemon juice
1 tbsp	15 ml	chopped fresh dill
		salt and freshly ground pepper
1 cup	250 ml	Diana Sauce, Fine Herbs with Lemon
4		kaiser rolls
4 tbsp	60 ml	butter
4 leaves		leaf lettuce

PUTTING ON THE GLOVES
Use a well-insulated barbecue mitt that extends well above the wrist to protect your arms from grease spatters and flare-ups. Remember, you're working with fire.

1. Season salmon fillets with barbecue seasoning, rubbing the spice into the flesh of the salmon.
2. Brush salmon fillets with oil.
3. In a bowl combine the apples, red onion, lemon juice, and dill. Season to taste with salt and pepper. Set aside.
4. Preheat grill to medium-high.
5. Grill salmon for 3–5 minutes per side, basting with Diana Sauce, until the fillets are cooked to medium and are lightly charred.
6. Cut each roll in half and brush with a tablespoon of butter and grill until slightly crisp.
7. Top one half of the roll with a fillet of grilled salmon. Add a ¼ cup (50 ml) of apple slaw.
8. Add a lettuce leaf and top with the other half of the roll.
9. Serve immediately.

Truck Stop Steak Sandwich

You won't find this recipe at a truck stop but you should. It's definitely designed for a big appetite. This is a steak sandwich like no other—smothered in Diana Sauce, Cracked Pepper. Scrumptious!

4 x 6 oz	165 g	sirloin steak
1 cup	250 ml	Diana's Marinade, Steak Spice
2 tbsp	25 ml	butter
1 medium		onion, diced
1 cup	250 ml	brown mushrooms, sliced
1 cup	250 ml	Diana Sauce, Cracked Pepper
		salt and freshly ground pepper
4		submarine rolls
1 cup	250 ml	crumbled blue cheese
8–12 slices		fresh tomato
4 leaves		fresh leaf lettuce

1. Place steaks in a glass dish and pour Diana's Steak Spice Marinade over, turning to coat evenly. Cover and refrigerate for 2–4 hours.
2. Melt the butter in a frying pan. Sauté the onions for 2–3 minutes until tender. Add the sliced mushrooms and continue to sauté for 5 minutes, stirring occasionally until the liquid has evaporated and the mushrooms are tender. Stir in ½ cup (125 ml) of Diana Sauce and season to taste with salt and pepper. Set aside, cover, and keep warm.
3. Remove steak from Diana's Marinade, discarding marinade.
4. Preheat grill to medium-high.
5. Grill steaks 4–5 minutes per side for medium-rare, basting with remaining ½ cup (125 ml) of Diana Sauce.
6. Remove steaks from grill and let stand for 5 minutes.
7. Slice buns in half lengthwise.

MARINADES AND SAUCES
Never reuse a marinade for a barbecue sauce because harmful bacteria from the meat can be passed to the food you are cooking. Always make a separate barbecue sauce or glaze and use clean utensils for serving.

8. Thinly slice each steak and place on the bottom half of a bun.
9. Top each steak with one-quarter of both the mushroom mixture and the crumbled blue cheese.
10. Garnish each sandwich with 2–3 slices of tomato and a lettuce leaf. Top with remaining half of bun.

HEAT OF THE MEAT

If you use a meat thermometer, here is a minimum temperature guide to follow:

Beef steaks, lamp chops	*145° F (63° C)*
Pork, kebabs, ground beef	*160° F (71° C)*
Poultry—dark meat	*180° F (82° C)*
Poultry—breast	*170° F (77° C)*

Sausage and Peppers Sandwich

If you enjoy the taste of sausage on a bun smothered in onions, then you'll love the flavour of this sausage that adds the zest of Heinz Chili Sauce and green bell peppers. Try it with either hot or sweet Italian sausage.

3 tbsp	45 ml	vegetable oil
2 cloves		garlic, minced
2 medium		onions, thickly sliced
1 large		red pepper, thickly sliced
1 large		green pepper, thickly sliced
¼ cup	50 ml	Heinz Tomato Ketchup
¼ cup	50 ml	Heinz Chili Sauce
2 tsp	10 ml	dry oregano
		salt and freshly ground pepper
6		hot or sweet Italian sausages
6		poppy seed rolls

1. In a large frying pan, heat the oil over medium-high heat. Sauté the garlic, onions, and peppers until tender, about 5–8 minutes.
2. Add Heinz Ketchup, Heinz Chili Sauce, and oregano, seasoning to taste with salt and pepper. Reduce heat to low and simmer, stirring occasionally, for 10 to 15 minutes.
3. Meanwhile, prepare the sausages as per package instructions until fully cooked.
4. Slice the rolls in half lengthwise and top each with a sausage and one-sixth of the onions and peppers.

Serves 6
Preparation time:
 15–20 minutes
Cooking time:
 25–30 minutes

Oregano
- A pungent odor and flavour
- Gives pizza its characteristic taste
- Indispensable in Italian, Greek, and Mexican cooking
- Ideal for grilled fish and meats, pork stews, slow-cooked vegetables, omelets, scrambled eggs, and soufflés
- Try sautéing vegetables in olive oil with garlic and oregano as a side dish

Remember: To release its flavour, crush oregano by hand or with a mortar and pestle before using it in your recipes.

Grilled Chicken Clubhouse with Canadian Bacon

Join the Canadian Club with this traditional clubhouse sandwich—a sandwich with a few extra ingredients that you wouldn't normally associate with this favourite. How does a slice of fresh grilled pineapple sound?

Serves 4
Marinade time: 2–4 hours
Preparation time:
  15 minutes
Grilling time: 20 minutes

4 x 6 oz	165 g	boneless, skinless chicken breasts
1 cup	250 ml	Diana's Marinade, Lemon and Pepper
1 cup	250 ml	Diana Sauce, Rib and Chicken
4 slices		fresh pineapple
4 slices		back bacon
4		sourdough rolls
4 slices		cheddar cheese
4 leaves		leaf lettuce
8 slices		beefsteak tomato, thinly sliced
1 small		red onion, thinly sliced

1. Place chicken breasts into a glass dish and pour Diana's Marinade over, turning to coat. Cover and refrigerate for 2–4 hours.
2. Preheat grill to medium-high.
3. Remove chicken from Diana's Lemon and Pepper Marinade, discarding marinade.
4. Grill chicken for 5–6 minutes per side, basting with Diana Sauce, until cooked through.
5. While the chicken is cooking, grill the pineapple and back bacon slices for 3–4 minutes per side. Set on top shelf of grill to keep warm.
6. Cut rolls in half and toast lightly. Set on top shelf of grill to keep warm.
7. When the chicken is cooked, set each breast on a slice of pineapple. Top each breast with back bacon and a slice of cheddar cheese. Close grill lid and cook for 3–4 minutes until cheese is melted.
8. Place each chicken stack on a roll and garnish with lettuce, tomato, and red onion.

CHECKING THE CHICKEN
Chicken can become dry and tasteless if overcooked on the grill. To check, cut into one of the pieces with a knife. The chicken is done if the juices run free and clearly. It is always best to use a meat thermometer and cook the chicken to 170˚.

Chili Cheese Dogs

The kids will love these chili cheese dogs because they're fun and messy. If you prefer to go vegetarian, you can substitute the ground beef with Yves Veggie Ground Round and the hot dogs with Yves Veggie Wieners.

Serves 6–8
Preparation time:
** 30 minutes**
Grilling time: 15 minutes

1 lb	454 g	regular ground beef
1 tbsp	15 ml	Heinz 57 BBQ Seasoning Rub (see page 11)
3 tbsp	45 ml	vegetable oil
1 small		onion, diced
1 can (14 oz)		Heinz Chili-Style Pinto and Red Kidney Beans
1½ cups	400 ml	Heinz Chili Sauce, Chunky with Sweet Peppers
6–8		jumbo hot dogs
6–8		hot dog rolls
1 cup	250 ml	grated cheddar cheese

THE COLOUR OF FIRE
The colour of your flame is a good indication of the health of your barbecue. The flame should be blue with a yellow tip. If the flame is too yellow or orange, you may have a blockage. Consult your owner's manual or call the manufacturer.

1. Season the beef with Heinz 57 BBQ Seasoning Rub.
2. In a frying pan, heat the oil over medium-high heat.
3. Sauté the beef with the onions until the liquid has evaporated and the onions are brown.
4. Add the pinto and kidney beans and Heinz Chili Sauce and bring mixture to a boil. Reduce heat to low and simmer for 10–15 minutes, stirring occasionally until chili mixture is fully cooked and thick. Set aside and keep warm.
5. Preheat grill to medium-high. Grill the hot dogs according to package instructions.
6. Lightly toast the hot dog rolls. Place one hot dog in a roll and pour a generous amount of chili over.
7. Top with grated cheddar cheese and serve.

Great Canadian Chicken Burger

While many chicken sandwiches use a grilled fillet, this recipe calls for ground chicken. The advantage of using ground chicken is the ability to add loads more seasoning and spices to the blend.

2 lbs	900 g	ground chicken
1 tbsp	15 ml	Heinz 57 BBQ Seasoning Rub (see page 11)
¼ cup	50 ml	Heinz Ketchup Kickers, Sweet Basil and Oregano
¼–½ cup	50–125 ml	breadcrumbs
1 lb.	454 g	bacon, fully cooked as per package instructions
8 slices		Swiss cheese
8		chipata buns or hamburger buns
4 cups	1 l	BBQ Coleslaw, (see page 30)

Makes 8 Burgers

Preparation Time: 20 minutes (not including burger-resting time)

Grill Time: 15–20 minutes

READINESS
Ground meats should always be cooked to the well-done stage, especially chicken or turkey.

1. In a large bowl combine ground chicken, barbecue seasoning, Heinz Ketchup Kickers, and breadcrumbs. Mix fully.
2. Portion the meat into eight 4-oz (125 g) burgers.
3. Form portions into uniform burger patties. Place each burger between sheets of parchment paper, cover with plastic wrap, and refrigerate for one hour to allow the meat to set.
4. Preheat grill to medium-high.
5. Grill the burgers for 5 to 6 minutes per side with the grill lid open, until fully cooked.
6. Top grilled burgers with cooked bacon and Swiss cheese, reduce grill heat to low, close lid, and allow the cheese to melt for 1 minute. At the same time toast your burger buns.
7. Place ½ cup (125 ml) of prepared coleslaw onto the base of each bun, top with bacon cheese chicken burgers, and garnish with your favourite burger toppings including Heinz Ketchup, Heinz Ketchup Kickers, mustard, and relish.

Great Canadian Bacon Cheeseburger

Why make regular burgers on the barbecue when you can grill up the Great Canadian Bacon Cheeseburger? With plenty of garnish and loads of Heinz Ketchup, Mustard and Relish, this is definitely a boastful burger. As a non-meat alternative, use Yves Veggie Burgers and Yves Veggie Canadian Bacon.

Makes 8 burgers
Preparation time: 20 minutes (not including burger-resting time)
Grill time: 15–20 minutes

2 lbs	900 g	regular ground beef
1 small		onion, finely diced
2 cloves		garlic, minced
1 tbsp	15 ml	chopped fresh parsley
1 tbsp	15 ml	Heinz Worcestershire Sauce
1 tbsp	15 ml	Heinz 57 BBQ Seasoning Rub (see page 11)
¼–⅓ cup	50–80 ml	Heinz Tomato Ketchup
8–16 slices		Canadian peameal bacon
8 slices		cheddar cheese
8		sesame seed burger buns

1. In a large bowl combine ground beef, onion, garlic, parsley, Worcestershire sauce, barbecue seasoning, and Heinz Ketchup. Mix fully.
2. Portion the meat into eight 4-oz (125 g) burgers.
3. Form portions into uniform burger patties. Place each burger between sheets of parchment paper, cover with plastic wrap, and refrigerate for one hour to allow the meat to set.
4. Preheat grill to medium-high.
5. Grill the burgers for 4 to 5 minutes per side with the grill lid open, until fully cooked.
6. While the burgers are cooking, grill the slices of peameal bacon for 2 to 3 minutes per side until fully cooked and tender.
7. Top grilled burgers with cooked peameal bacon and cheese, reduce grill heat to low, close lid, and allow the cheese to melt for 1 minute. At the same time toast your burger buns.

BASHING THE BURGER
How many times have you seen someone use a spatula to press down on a burger as it's being cooked? That's a no-no. Pressing down squeezes out the natural juices and creates a dry and burnt-tasting burger.

8. Top each bun with bacon cheese burgers and garnish with your favourite burger toppings including Heinz Ketchup, mustard, and relish

Grilled Beef

Grilled New York Peppercorn Steak

Grilled 57 Flank Steak Fajitas

Grilled New York Striploin Steaks with Sweet
  and Sour Onions

Steakhouse T-Bone with Grilled Red Onions

Ginger Teriyaki Beef and Vegetable Kebabs

Bloody Mary-Grilled Sirloin Steaks

Roasted Garlic Rib Steak with Stilton Cheese
  and a Bourbon BBQ Sauce

Grilled New York Peppercorn Steak

The classic peppercorn steak is a revered steakhouse specialty. Tender aged beef striploin steaks rubbed with cracked black pepper will showcase your grilling skills.

¼ cup	50 ml	coarsely cracked black peppercorns
4 cloves		garlic, minced
4 x 12 oz	375 g	New York striploin steaks, about 1½ inch (3.5 cm) thick
1 cup	250 ml	Diana's Marinade, Steak Spice
1 cup	250 ml	Diana Sauce, Cracked Pepper

Serves 4
Marinade time: 2–4 hours
Preparation time:
  20 minutes
Grilling time:
  8–10 minutes for
  medium doneness

1. In a small bowl combine the coarsely ground black peppercorns and garlic. Rub the pepper and garlic mixture into the steaks, pressing the spices into the meat.
2. Place the steaks on a flat glass baking dish. Pour the Diana's Steak Spice Marinade over steaks, turning to coat evenly. Cover and refrigerate for 2–4 hours.
3. Preheat grill to medium-high.
4. Remove steaks from Diana's Marinade and discard marinade.
5. Grill steaks for 4–5 minutes per side for medium doneness, basting liberally with Diana Sauce.
6. Remove steaks from grill and allow meat to rest for 5 minutes.

PREVENTING FLARE-UPS
Flare-ups are a sign of a poorly cleaned grill or food with a lot of fat. Always have a spray bottle of water at hand to lightly spritz any flames. For larger flare-ups, turn off the gas and close the lid to smother the flames. Clean your grill regularly and always have a fire extinguisher readily available.

Grilled 57 Flank Steak Fajitas

Say olé to this Tex/Mex original, which will wake anyone from a siesta. No ordinary fajita, this recipe features a marinade and sauce that will bring your steak to life.

Serves 4
Marinade time: 4 hours
Preparation time:
  20 minutes
Grilling time: 10 minutes

Marinade

1½ lbs	675 g	beef flank steak
1 cup	250 ml	Diana's Marinade, Steak Spice
1 tbsp	15 ml	Heinz 57 BBQ Seasoning Rub (see page 11)

Barbecue Sauce

½ cup	125 ml	Heinz 57 Sauce
½ cup	125 ml	Diana Sauce, Cracked Pepper
2 tbsp	25 ml	Heinz Pure Malt Vinegar
1 tbsp	15 ml	chopped fresh cilantro

Fajita Garnish

8 inch	17.5 cm	flour tortillas
2 cups	500 ml	shredded iceberg lettuce
1 cup	250 ml	sour cream
1 cup	250 ml	guacamole
1 cup	250 ml	salsa
1 cup	250 ml	grated cheddar cheese

MARINADES
Marinades are used to tenderize and flavourize meats. They consist of three basic elements: oils, acids, and flavourings. Oil can be any type of oil. Acids usually have vinegar as a main ingredient but can also include any type of fruit juice. Flavourings include spices and herbs. Always add vinegar to marinades first, then gradually mix in the oil to ensure proper blending.

1. Using a sharp knife, trim the flank steak of excess fat and sinew.
2. Score the beef on either side about ¼ inch (0.70 cm) deep in a diamond pattern. Place in a glass dish.
3. Pour Diana's Steak Spice Marinade over, cover, and refrigerate for 4–6 hours.
4. While the steak is marinating, prepare the barbecue sauce. In a bowl whisk together the Heinz 57 sauce, Diana Sauce, vinegar, and cilantro. Set aside and refrigerate.
5. Preheat grill to medium-high.

6. Remove steak from Diana's Marinade, discarding marinade, and season with barbecue seasoning on both sides.
7. Grill steak for 3–5 minutes per side for medium-rare doneness, basting with prepared barbecue sauce.
8. Remove steak from grill and allow to rest for 5 minutes.
9. Thinly slice the steak on the bias and serve with warmed flour tortillas, shredded lettuce, sour cream, guacamole, salsa, and grated cheddar cheese.

Grilled New York Striploin Steaks with Sweet and Sour Onions

Start spreading the news, because this New York steak recipe puts a whole new twist on fried onions. It's a sweet and sour onion mixture that's easy to make with prepared products from Heinz. Make this dish for your next get-together, and your guests will be singing your praises.

4 x 12 oz	375 g	New York striploin steaks, cut about 1½ inch (3.5 cm) thick
1 cup	250 ml	Diana's Marinade, Steak Spice

Sweet and Sour Onions

3 tbsp	45 ml	butter
4 cloves		garlic, minced
2 large		onions, sliced
1 tbsp	15 ml	Heinz Worcestershire Sauce
¼ cup	50 ml	Heinz Pure Malt Vinegar
½ cup	125 ml	Heinz Chili Sauce
1 cup	250 ml	Heinz Tomato Ketchup
2 tbsp	25 ml	chopped parsley
		salt and freshly ground pepper

Serves 4
Marinade time: 2–4 hours
Preparation time:
  30 minutes
Grilling time: 10 minutes

DONE LIKE DINNER

To test the doneness of steaks, chops, and burgers simply do the touch test. Rare meat gives easily. Medium feels slightly springy, and juices appear on the surface. Well-done meat has no running juices and is firm to the touch.

1. Fit the steaks into the bottom of a glass dish. Pour the Diana's Steak Spice Marinade over the meat, and turn to coat evenly. Cover and refrigerate for 2–4 hours.
2. While the steaks are marinating, prepare the sweet and sour onions.
3. Heat butter in a large frying pan. Add garlic and onions and sauté for 6–8 minutes, stirring until tender and slightly golden brown. Reduce heat to medium and add Worcestershire sauce, vinegar, Heinz Chili Sauce, and Heinz Ketchup and continue to cook, stirring, for 4–5 minutes. Add parsley and season to taste with salt and pepper. Set aside and keep warm.
4. Preheat grill to medium-high.
5. Remove steaks from Diana's Marinade, discarding marinade.
6. Grill steaks for 4–5 minutes per side for medium doneness. Remove steaks from grill and allow to rest for 5 minutes. Thinly slice each steak on the bias and serve with the sweet and sour onions.

Steakhouse T-Bone with Grilled Red Onions

The T-bone is a fine cut of meat. It gives the choice to two wonderful cuts: the striploin and the tenderloin. This is a perfect steak for sharing especially when the cut is nice and thick.

2 x 1 lb	454 g	T-bone steaks, cut about 1½ inches (3.5 cm) thick
1 cup	250 ml	Diana's Marinade, Steak Spice
2 tbsp	25 ml	Heinz 57 BBQ Seasoning Rub (see page 11)
2 large		red onions, cut into 1 inch (2.5 cm) slices
1 bottle		Heinz 57 Sauce
1 tbsp	15 ml	Heinz Worcestershire Sauce
½ cup	125 ml	Heinz Ketchup Kickers, Roasted Garlic
2 tbsp	25 ml	vegetable oil
		salt and freshly ground pepper

Serves 2–4
Marinade time: 2–4 hours
Preparation time: 20 minutes
Grilling time: 20 minutes

TRIMMING FAT
Trim the fat and skin from steaks and chicken after cooking. The fat and skin produce natural juices that baste the food while it cooks.

1. Fit the steaks into the bottom of a glass dish. Pour the Diana's Steak Spice Marinade over the meat, turning to coat evenly. Cover and refrigerate for 2–4 hours.
2. Place the onion slices in another glass dish in an even layer. Season onions with barbecue seasoning on both sides.
3. In a bowl whisk together the Heinz 57 sauce, Worcestershire sauce, Heinz Ketchup Kickers, and vegetable oil. Pour half of this mixture over the onions and marinate for 1 hour. Reserve remaining sauce for the grill.
4. Preheat grill to medium-high.
5. Remove steaks from Diana'a Marinade, discarding marinade, and grill for 5 minutes per side for medium doneness, basting liberally with reserved sauce.
6. While the steaks are cooking, grill the onions for 2–3 minutes per side until lightly charred and tender. Transfer the onions to the top shelf of the grill to keep warm.
7. Remove steaks from grill and let rest for 5 minutes.
8. Serve with grilled onions.

Ginger Teriyaki Beef and Vegetable Kebabs

The Japanese created one of the world's greatest flavours—the incredible taste of teriyaki. The Japanese also love ginger, and most commonly use it in sushi. We've married these two flavours—and introduced a Greek element, kebabs—to create a recipe that knows no borders.

Serves 8
Marinade time: 2–4 hours
Preparation time:
  30 minutes
Grilling time: 15 minutes

16		10 inch (25 cm) metal skewers
4 lbs	2 kg	beef sirloin, cut into 2 x 2-inch (5 x 5 cm) cubes
2 cups	500 ml	Diana's Marinade, Teriyaki
2 tbsp	25 ml	olive oil
2 tbsp	25 ml	chopped fresh ginger
4 cloves		garlic, minced
1 tbsp	15 ml	chopped fresh cilantro
2 tbsp	25 ml	dijon mustard
2 tsp	10 ml	cracked black peppercorns
2		green zucchini
2		red peppers
2		yellow peppers
2 medium		red onions, peeled
24 large		mushrooms
¼ cup	50 ml	corn syrup
½ cup	125 ml	Heinz Tomato Ketchup
1 tbsp	15 ml	Heinz Worcestershire Sauce
2 tbsp	25 ml	Heinz Pure Apple Cider Vinegar
2		green onions, minced
		salt and freshly ground pepper

HOT HANDS
When grilling kebabs on metal skewers, wear insulated mitts. It doesn't take long for the heat of the grill to travel to the end of the skewer.

1. In a large bowl toss the beef with 1 cup of the Diana's Teriyaki Marinade, olive oil, ginger, garlic, cilantro, mustard, and black pepper. Cover and refrigerate for 2–4 hours.
2. Remove beef from Diana's Marinade, discarding marinade, and thread onto 8 skewers. (Note, if using bamboo skewers, soak them in warm water for at least 1 hour prior to threading meat.)

3. Cut zucchini, red and yellow peppers and red onions into large pieces. Skewer the vegetables and mushrooms onto 8 skewers.
4. In a bowl combine the remaining cup of Diana's Teriyaki Marinade, corn syrup, Heinz Ketchup, Worcestershire sauce, and vinegar. Season to taste with salt and pepper.
5. Preheat grill to medium-high.
6. Grill beef skewers for 2–3 minutes per side (total: 8–12 minutes) for medium-rare, basting with teriyaki basting sauce.
7. After the beef has cooked for 3 minutes, place the vegetable skewers on the grill and cook for 6–8 minutes, until tender, basting with teriyaki basting sauce.
8. Remove from grill and serve.

Bloody Mary-Grilled Sirloin Steaks

Not many people can pass up the taste of a Bloody Mary. Well, there's no reason poor Mary must be confined to the bar, because we've turned the cocktail into a marinade for sirloin steaks. It's a recipe that's sure to have your guests ordering a second round.

Serves 4
Marinade time: 4 hours
Preparation time:
  15 minutes
Grilling time: 15 minutes

1 tbsp	15 ml	Heinz Worcestershire Sauce
½ cup	125 ml	Diana's Marinade, Steak Spice
½ cup	125 ml	Heinz Ketchup Kickers, Hot and Spicy
1 cup	250 ml	Heinz Tomato Juice
2 oz	60 ml	vodka
4 x 8 oz	225 g	beef sirloin steaks
		salt and freshly ground pepper

Tomatoes get their taste from a substance called furenol that develops during the ripening process. This is why tomatoes need to ripen before they taste good.

1. In a bowl whisk together the Worcestershire sauce, Diana's Steak Spice Marinade, Heinz Ketchup Kickers, tomato juice, and vodka.
2. Fit sirloin steaks into a glass dish and pour half of the Bloody Mary mixture over the meat, reserving the remainder for the grill.
3. Cover and refrigerate steaks for 4 hours.
4. Remove steaks from Diana's Marinade, discarding marinade, and season to taste with salt and pepper.
5. Preheat grill to medium-high.
6. Grill steaks for 4–5 minutes per side for medium doneness, basting liberally with reserved Bloody Mary mixture.
7. Remove steaks from grill, allowing to rest for 5 minutes.
8. Serve immediately with mashed potatoes and grilled vegetables—and maybe a Bloody Mary or two.

Roasted Garlic Rib Steak with Stilton Cheese and a Bourbon BBQ Sauce

Serves 4
Preparation time:
 15 minutes
Grilling time: 10 minutes

The rib steak and the filet are the most tender cuts of beef. When purchasing this cut, look for well-marbled steaks that are at least 1½ inch (3.5 cm) thick. Try adding some extra flavour by using Diana's Steak Spice Marinade, to marinate the steaks in the refrigerator for 2–4 hours.

4 x 12 oz	375 g	boneless rib steak, about 1½ inches (3.5 cm) thick
2 tbsp	25 ml	Heinz 57 BBQ Seasoning Rub (see page 11)
1 tbsp	15 ml	chopped fresh rosemary
¼ cup	50 ml	honey
2 oz	60 ml	bourbon
1 cup	250 ml	Heinz Ketchup Kickers, Roasted Garlic
½ cup	125 ml	crumbled Stilton cheese

1. Rub the rib steaks with barbecue seasoning, pressing the spices into the meat.
2. In a bowl whisk together the rosemary, honey, bourbon, and Heinz Ketchup Kickers. Set aside.
3. Preheat grill to medium-high.
4. Grill steaks for 4–5 minutes per side for medium doneness, basting liberally with sauce mixture.
5. Remove steaks from grill and allow to rest for 5 minutes.
6. Top each steak with crumbled blue cheese. Serve with sautéed mushrooms and onions.

Grilled Pork And Lamb

Maple BBQ Back Ribs

Asian Glazed Butterflied Pork Tenderloin

Spiced Maple BBQ Pork Chops

Roasted Garlic Lamb Chops

Grilled Kielbasa Sausage with Curry BBQ Sauce

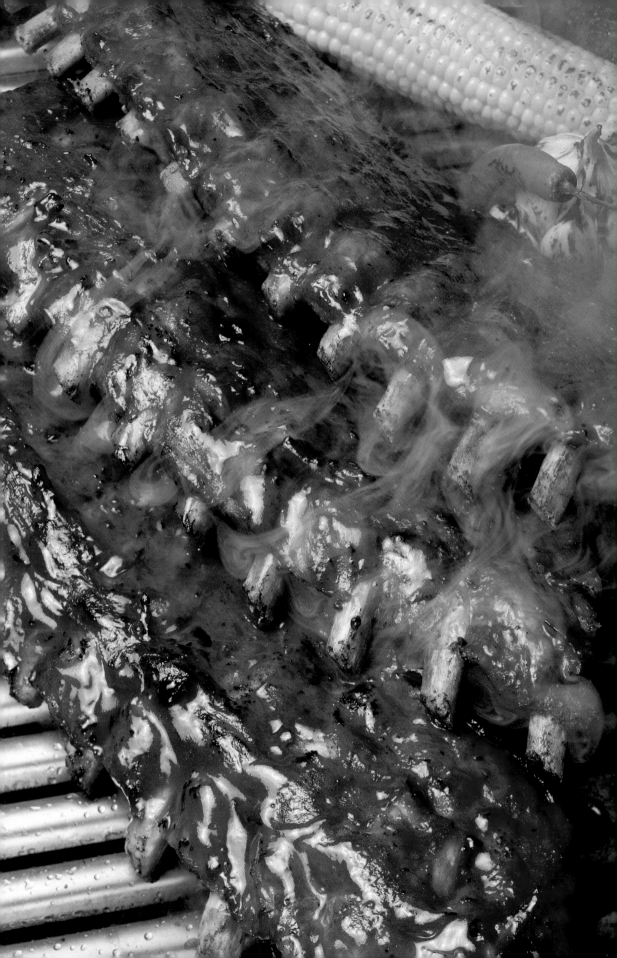

Maple BBQ Back Ribs

The natural sweetness of maple syrup gives this dish a taste not often associated with ribs. These barbecued back ribs leap off the grill with Diana Rib and Chicken Sauce. Definitely a melt-in-your-mouth experience. Have lots of wet towels handy and perhaps even a bib!

Serves 4–6
Preparation time:
  2–2½ hours
Grilling time:
  15–20 minutes

2–3 1½ lb	675 g	baby back rib racks
2 tbsp	25 ml	Heinz 57 BBQ Seasoning Rub (see page 11)
1 large		yellow onion, sliced
½ cup	125 ml	Diana's Marinade, Garlic and Herbs
2 cans		ginger ale
2		lemons, thinly sliced
½ cup	125 ml	maple syrup
1½ cups	375 ml	Diana Sauce, Rib and Chicken

CATCHING THE DRIPS
Use an an old cake pan and fasten it below the grill to catch the grease and juices as you cook. Be sure to wash it in hot soapy water after every use.

1. Using a sharp knife, score the membrane on the back of the ribs several times. Rub with barbecue seasoning, pressing the seasoning into the meat.
2. Preheat oven to 325°F (160°C).
3. Place the onions in the bottom of a 3 inch (7 cm) deep roasting pan.
4. Place the ribs meat side down on top of the onions. Place 3–4 slices of lemon on the back of each rib. Mix together the Diana's Garlic and Herbs Marinade and ginger ale and pour into the bottom of the pan and cover.
5. Braise ribs in oven for 2–2½ hours until tender. Remove from oven and let cool slightly. Carefully remove ribs from pan, discarding braising liquid.
6. In a bowl combine the maple syrup and Diana Sauce.
7. Preheat grill to medium-high.
8. Grill ribs for 6–8 minutes per side, basting with the mixture of maple syrup and Diana Sauce.
9. Cut between every third rib and serve.

Asian Glazed Butterflied Pork Tenderloin

Serves 3–4
Marinade time: 2 hours
Preparation time:
  30 minutes
Grilling time:
  10–15 minutes

Pork is a delicious meat for grilling, and this recipe first marinates pork tenderloin in Diana's Teriyaki Marinade. Accompanying a sweet barbecue sauce inspired by an Asian theme, this butterflied pork tenderloin is a lean dish that will add excitement to your dinner party menu.

Marinade

1 x 1½ lbs	675 g	pork tenderloin, trimmed of excess fat and sinew
1½ cup	375 ml	Diana's Marinade, Teriyaki

Barbecue Sauce

¼ cup	50 ml	pineapple juice
½ cup	125 ml	Heinz Tomato Ketchup
2 tbsp	25 ml	brown sugar
1 tbsp	15 ml	minced ginger
2 tsp	10 ml	sesame seeds
2 tsp	10 ml	crushed red chilies
2		green onions, finely chopped
		salt and freshly ground pepper

1. Using a sharp knife, make an incision the length of the pork tenderloin about ¾ inch (2 cm) deep. Using the tip of the knife, carefully make a butterfly incision on either side of your initial cut the length of the pork. Repeat.

2. Place the pork tenderloin between two sheets of plastic wrap and lightly pound with a meat mallet to a uniform thickness of ½ inch (1 cm) to 1 inch (2.5 cm).

3. Place pork tenderloin in a glass dish and pour 1 cup (250 ml) of Diana's Marinade over, tuning to coat evenly. Cover and refrigerate for 2 hours.

4. In a saucepan, combine the remaining ½ cup (125 ml) of Diana's Teriyaki Marinade, pineapple juice, Heinz Ketchup, brown sugar, ginger, sesame seeds, chilies, and green onions. Season to taste with salt

and pepper. Bring sauce to a boil, reduce heat, and simmer for 10 minutes, stirring occasionally. Remove from heat and set aside.

5. Preheat grill to medium-high.
6. Remove pork tenderloin from Diana's Marinade, discarding marinade.
7. Grill pork for 4–5 minutes per side for medium-well doneness, basting with pineapple barbecue sauce.
8. Remove from grill and let the meat stand for 5 minutes. Thinly slice pork across the grain of the meat.

BASTING

If you've used a dry rub before barbecuing, always allow the meat to cook for approximately one-third to one-half the total time before applying any basting sauce. This cooking time will allow the meat to warm and start absorbing the dry rub seasonings. If you begin to baste too early you will be "washing off" the dry rub seasonings. After the "warmup," you may baste as frequently as you wish (but probably not more often than every 20 minutes).

Spiced Maple BBQ Pork Chops

These are quick barbecue pork chops that take only 30 minutes to prepare. The sweetness of the maple syrup combined with Diana's Steak Spice Marinade and Heinz Ketchup Kickers, Hot and Spicy gives this pork dish indescribable flavour.

Serves 6
Marinade time: 4 hours
Preparation time:
  30 minutes
Grilling time: 20 minutes

Marinade

6 x 8 oz	225 g	pork chops, cut 1½ inches (3.5 cm) thick
1 cup	250 ml	Diana's Marinade, Steak Spice
1 tbsp	15 ml	Heinz 57 BBQ Seasoning Rub (see page 11)

Barbecue Sauce

2 cloves		garlic, minced
¼ cup	50 ml	maple syrup
½ cup	125 ml	Heinz Ketchup Kickers, Hot and Spicy
1 cup	250 ml	Diana Sauce, Original
1 tbsp	15 ml	Heinz Worcestershire Sauce
1 tbsp	15 ml	chopped fresh thyme

Mop Top

Many sauces are applied to food with a food mop. These are available in the housewares section of your hardware store.

1. Place pork chops in a glass dish. Pour Diana's Steak Spice Marinade over chops, turning to coat evenly. Cover and refrigerate for 4 hours.
2. In a saucepan, combine the garlic, maple syrup, Heinz Ketchup Kickers, Diana Sauce, Worcestershire sauce, and thyme. Bring mixture slowly to a boil, reduce heat, and simmer for 10 minutes, stirring occasionally. Remove from heat and set aside.
3. Remove pork chops from Diana's Marinade, discarding marinade.
4. Preheat grill to medium-high.
5. Grill pork chops for 6–8 minutes per side, basting with spicy maple barbecue sauce.
6. Remove from grill and serve with coleslaw.

Roasted Garlic Lamb Chops

Succulent lamb chops taste great when grilled on the barbecue, and the sweet barbecue sauce used in this recipe brings out the natural sweetness of the lamb.

Serves 6–9
Marinade time: 2–4 hours
Preparation time:
  15 minutes
Grilling time:
  15–20 minutes

18		lamb chops, cut 1½ inches (3.5 cm) thick
1½ cups	375 ml	Diana's Marinade, Garlic and Herbs
¼ cup	50 ml	honey
½ cup	125 ml	Heinz Ketchup Kickers, Roasted Garlic
1 cup	250 ml	Heinz Western Grill Garlic BBQ Sauce
2 tsp	10 ml	cracked black pepper
1 tbsp	15 ml	chopped fresh rosemary
		salt

1. Place lamb chops in a glass dish and pour Diana's Marinade over, turning once. Cover and refrigerate for 2–4 hours.
2. In a bowl whisk together the honey, Heinz Ketchup Kickers, Heinz Barbecue Sauce, black pepper, and rosemary. Season to taste with salt.
3. Preheat grill to medium-high.
4. Remove lamb chops from Diana's Marinade, discarding marinade.
5. Grill lamb chops for 5–6 minutes per side for medium-rare doneness, basting with roasted garlic barbecue sauce.
6. Serve 2–3 chops per person with mashed potatoes and grilled vegetables.

Rosemary
- Part of the mint family with tea-like aroma and piney flavour
- Used primarily in lamb, pork, chicken, and rabbit dishes
- An ancient spice prized for its value as incense and memory enhancer
- Crush and sprinkle on grilled vegetables and meats, particularly roast lamb, chicken, and game
- Livens up marinades, potatoes, onions, stuffed vegetables, and savoury jellies

Remember: When grilling, rub spices into meat before cooking.

Grilled Kielbasa Sausage with Curry BBQ Sauce

Serves 6–8
Preparation time:
 15 minutes
Grilling time: 20 minutes

Direct from Germany, this recipe for kielbasa sausage has a twist of curry and garlic. This is a sausage-fest worth celebrating. Prosit!

2 tbsp	25 ml	vegetable oil
3 cloves		garlic, minced
1 small		yellow onion, diced
2–3 tsp	10–15 ml	curry powder
¼ cup	50 ml	Heinz Tomato Ketchup
½ cup	125 ml	Heinz Chili Sauce
1 cup	250 ml	Heinz Western Grill Original BBQ Sauce
		salt and freshly ground pepper
1½ lbs	675 g	pork kielbasa coil

To release ketchup from your glass bottle faster, tap the "57" on the neck of the bottle. If you apply one firm tap where the bottle narrows, the ketchup will come out more easily.

1. In a small saucepan, heat the oil over medium heat. Sauté the garlic and onion for 2 minutes, stirring, until tender. Add the curry powder and continue to cook for 1 minute longer, stirring.
2. Add the Heinz Ketchup, Heinz Chili Sauce, and Heinz Barbecue Sauce. Bring to a boil, reduce heat, and simmer for 10 minutes, stirring occasionally.
3. Remove from heat.
4. Preheat grill to medium-high.
5. Place kielbasa coil on grill and cook for 2–3 minutes per side until slightly charred.
6. Reduce grill heat to medium-low and close lid. Grill kielbasa for 8–10 minutes, turning occasionally.
7. Open grill lid and cut the kielbasa halfway through, approximately every ½ inch (1 cm).
8. Baste the cuts liberally with the curry barbecue sauce and grill for 5 more minutes until the kielbasa is crisp.
9. Slice through every third slash and serve with sauerkraut and beer.

Grilled Poultry

Honey Balsamic-Grilled Chicken Thighs

Canadian Grilled Bacon-Wrapped Drumsticks

Grilled Mango Chicken

Heinz Cordon Bleu Grilled Chicken Breasts
  Stuffed with Ham and Brie Cheese

Honey Mustard BBQ Chicken

Orange BBQ Turkey Steaks

Diana's Grilled Rosemary Chicken

Honey Balsamic-Grilled Chicken Thighs

Some people like the breast of a chicken; others swear by chicken drumsticks. However, many chefs will tell you that the chicken thigh is the tastiest part of the bird. Try venturing into thigh territory with this recipe featuring Heinz Ketchup Kickers, Roasted Garlic.

Serves 4–6
Marinade time: 2–4 hours
Preparation time:
  15 minutes
Grilling time:
  30–40 minutes

Marinade

| 12 | | chicken thighs |
| 1½ cups | 400 ml | Diana's Marinade, Garlic and Herbs |

Honey Balsamic Sauce

1 tbsp	15 ml	chopped fresh rosemary
2 tbsp	25 ml	vegetable oil
¼ cup	50 ml	balsamic vinegar
½ cup	125 ml	honey
1 cup	250 ml	Heinz Ketchup Kickers, Roasted Garlic
		salt and freshly ground pepper

1. Place chicken thighs in a glass dish and pour Diana's Garlic and Herbs Marinade over, turning to coat evenly. Cover and refrigerate for 2–4 hours.
2. Meanwhile, prepare the honey balsamic sauce by mixing together the rosemary, oil, vinegar, honey, and Heinz Ketchup Kickers. Season to taste with salt and pepper.
3. Preheat grill to medium.
4. Remove chicken from Diana's Marinade, discarding marinade, and grill for 3–4 minutes per side to lightly char. Reduce heat to medium-low and close grill lid. Cook thighs for 30–40 minutes, basting occasionally with honey balsamic sauce.
5. Serve immediately.

Canadian Grilled Bacon-Wrapped Drumsticks

Serves 4–6
Preparation time:
  15 minutes
Grilling time:
  45–60 minutes

It's dress-up time for the good old chicken drumstick. The bacon becomes the chicken's second skin—making this dish perfect for a picnic or as an appetizer or finger food. The flavours of Diana Sauce and Heinz Worcestershire Sauce will have your guests beating the drum for more of this fabulous chicken.

CORN SMOKE
If you want to add a delicious smoky flavour to your grilled food, use corn on the cob. Simply dry out a few cobs of corn (without the corn) in the sun, cut them into smaller chunks, and put them in a special barbecue-smoking box on the grill.

12		chicken drumsticks or thighs
3 tbsp	45 ml	Heinz 57 BBQ Seasoning Rub (see page 11)
12 slices		bacon
12		toothpicks
24		whole cloves
1 tbsp	15 ml	Heinz Worcestershire Sauce
½ cup	125 ml	maple syrup
½ cup	125 ml	Heinz Tomato Ketchup
1 cup	250 ml	Diana Sauce, Original
4 cloves		garlic, minced
1 tbsp	15 ml	chopped fresh thyme
1–2 tbsp	15–25 ml	lemon juice
		salt and pepper

1. Season the chicken pieces with barbecue seasoning, pressing the seasoning into the meat.
2. Partially cook the bacon slices in a large frying pan until the fat begins to render. Remove bacon and drain on paper towel.
3. Roll each piece of chicken in a slice of bacon and secure with a toothpick. Insert one to two whole cloves into each piece of chicken.
4. In a bowl, mix together the Worcestershire sauce, maple syrup, Heinz Ketchup, Diana Sauce, garlic, thyme, and lemon juice. Season to taste with salt and pepper.
5. Preheat grill to medium.

6. Grill the bacon-wrapped chicken drumsticks for 2–3 minutes per side to lightly char. Reduce grill heat to low and close grill lid. Slowly grill the chicken for 30–40 minutes while basting occasionally with maple/ketchup mixture, until the chicken is fully cooked and the bacon is crisp.
7. Remove toothpicks and serve immediately.

Grilled Mango Chicken

Mangoes are often overlooked; many people don't know how to use this deliciously sweet fruit. This recipe for grilled chicken features tropical flavours such as mango, orange, lemon, and lime—giving the dish a refreshing zestiness.

Serves 4
Marinade time: 2–4 hours
Preparation time:
  20 minutes
Grilling time:
  15–20 minutes

EXTRA GUESTS
If you find you have extra mouths to feed, turn your steaks or chicken into kebabs or fajitas. That way you'll be able to stretch the food further.

Marinade

4 x 6 oz	150 g	chicken breasts, boneless and skinless
½ cup	125 ml	Diana's Marinade, Lemon and Pepper
½ cup	125 ml	orange juice

Barbecue Sauce

1 ripe		mango, peeled and diced
2		green onions, chopped
1 tbsp	15 ml	chopped fresh cilantro
2 tbsp	25 ml	olive oil
1		lime, juiced
½ cup	125 ml	Heinz Chili Sauce, Chunky with Sweet Peppers
¼ cup	50 ml	Heinz Ketchup Kickers, Hot and Spicy
		salt and freshly ground pepper

1. Place chicken in a glass dish, and pour Diana's Lemon and Pepper Marinade and orange juice over. Cover and refrigerate for 2–4 hours.
2. Meanwhile, prepare the mango sauce in a food processor or blender. Combine the mango, green onion, cilantro, olive oil, lime juice, Heinz Chili Sauce, and Heinz Ketchup Kickers. Blend until smooth. Transfer sauce to a glass container.
3. Preheat grill to medium-high.
4. Remove chicken from Diana's Marinade, discarding marinade, and grill for 5–6 minutes, basting with mango sauce, until the chicken is fully cooked.
5. Remove from grill and serve with sliced fresh mango.

Heinz Cordon Bleu Grilled Chicken Breasts Stuffed with Ham and Brie Cheese

In the great Cordon Bleu tradition, this cut of chicken is a work of art—a boneless breast skin-on with the wing drummette bone attached. To enjoy this dish ask your butcher to prepare foodservice-style chicken breast supremes. Since the breast is boneless it's perfect for a delicious stuffing of brie and Black Forest ham.

Serves 8
Preparation time:
  1½ hours
Grilling time: 20 minutes

6 x 8 oz	225 g	chicken breasts, boneless with skin on
½ cup	125 ml	Heinz 57 BBQ Seasoning Rub (see page 11)
½ cup	125 g	brie
½ cup	125 ml	Heinz Chili Sauce
1 tsp	5 ml	Heinz Worcestershire Sauce
2		green onions, finely chopped
1 tsp	5 ml	coarsely ground black pepper
1 tbsp	15 ml	Heinz Red Wine Flavoured Vinegar
1 tbsp	15 ml	chopped fresh thyme
		salt
6 slices		Black Forest ham
1 cup	250 ml	Diana Sauce, Honey Garlic

1. Place the chicken breasts skin side down on a flat work surface. Remove the chicken tenderloin and set aside. Using a sharp knife, make an incision ½-inch (1.25 cm) deep from the top of the breast to the bottom.
2. Using the tip of the knife, carefully make a butterfly incision on either side of your initial cut. Use your fingers to make a large pocket. Season the chicken breasts inside and out with barbecue seasoning.
3. Lightly pound the chicken tenderloins until flat.

Tarragon

- A slightly bittersweet flavour and an aroma similar to licorice
- Adds flavour to egg and cheese dishes, light soups, and fresh fruits
- To baste chicken, fish, or seafood, blend tarragon with melted butter, chives, and lemon
- Commonly used as a flavouring for vinegar and in pickles, relishes, prepared mustards, and sauces

Remember: To substitute dried herb for fresh, use about half the amount.

4. In a food processor or blender, mix together the brie, Heinz Chili Sauce, Worcestershire sauce, green onions, pepper, vinegar, and thyme. Blend until smooth and season to taste with salt.
5. Divide the brie stuffing into six portions and form each portion into an oval shape.
6. Wrap each stuffing portion with a slice of Black Forest ham.
7. Place one ham roll into the cavity of each chicken.
8. Place the flat tenderloins over the top of the ham roll, and tuck all edges into the cavity; press firmly to make a tight seal. Cover and refrigerate for 1 hour.
9. Preheat grill to medium-high.
10. Grill the chicken for 6–8 minutes per side starting with the skin side down. Toward the end of the grilling time, baste with Diana Sauce.
11. Serve immediately.

Honey Mustard BBQ Chicken

This recipe calls for all the parts from a whole chicken and is designed to please everyone. You will have two breasts, two wings, two thighs, and two drumsticks—each with the distinct flavour of honey and mustard.

Serves 4
Marinade time: 2–4 hours
Grilling time:
  30–40 minutes
Preparation time:
  15 minutes

Marinade

1 whole		chicken (about 3–4 lbs/1.5–2 kg), cut into 8 pieces
1½ cups	400 ml	Diana's Marinade, Lemon and Pepper

Barbecue Sauce

4 cloves		garlic, minced
¼ cup	50 ml	honey
¼ cup	50 ml	Heinz Prepared Mustard
½ cup	125 ml	Diana Sauce, Rib and Chicken
1 tbsp	25 ml	chopped cilantro
		salt and freshly ground pepper to taste

SPIDER INSIDER
The venturi tubes that connect your grill to the control knobs may become a nesting area for insects and spiders. At least twice a year, clean the tubes and other parts of your barbecue to get rid of the spider insiders.

1. Place chicken parts in a glass dish and pour Diana's Lemon and Pepper Marinade over, turning to coat evenly. Cover and refrigerate for 2–4 hours.
2. Preheat grill to medium-high.
3. To create the honey mustard sauce, combine Diana Sauce, mustard, honey, garlic and cilantro and set aside.
4. Remove chicken pieces from Diana's Marinade, discarding marinade, and grill for 4–5 minutes per side.
5. Reduce heat to medium-low and continue to cook for 20–30 minutes with the lid closed, occasionally basting with the honey mustard sauce.

Orange BBQ Turkey Steaks

Serves 6
Preparation time:
   30 minutes
Grilling time:
   20 minutes
Marinating time:
   2–4 hours

Turkey for Christmas. Turkey for Thanksgiving. For most people, that about sums it up for turkey. Turkeys are always available through your butcher or grocer and they deserve more attention all year round. This recipe bathes the turkey steaks in the sweet flavours of the orange both in the marinade and in the barbecue sauce used to baste on the grill.

Marinade

1 x 2 lbs	900 g	turkey breast, boneless and skinless
3 tbsp	45 ml	Heinz 57 BBQ Seasoning Rub (see page 11)
½ cup	125 ml	Diana's Marinade, Garlic and Herbs
1 cup	250 ml	orange juice

Barbecue Sauce

2 tbsp	25 ml	vegetable oil
1 small		onion, diced
½ cup	125 ml	orange juice
1 cup	250 ml	Diana Sauce, Original
1 tbsp	15 ml	brown sugar
1 tbsp	15 ml	Heinz Pure Apple Cider Vinegar
1 tbsp	15 ml	chopped fresh dill

1. Using a sharp knife, slice the turkey breast on the bias (across the breast) into six or eight 1-inch (2.5 cm) slices.
2. Mix the barbecue seasoning, marinade, and orange juice. Place turkey steaks in a glass dish, and pour the marinade over, turning once to coat. Cover and refrigerate for 2–4 hours.
3. In a saucepan, heat the oil. Sauté the onion for 3 minutes until tender. Add the orange juice, Diana Sauce, brown sugar, vinegar, and dill. Bring to a

Cumin

- A distinctive, slightly bitter yet warm flavour
- One of the world's ancient spices
- Mentioned in the Old Testament
- An important spice in Mexican and Indian cuisine
- Adds zest when added to lemon-based marinades for chicken, turkey, lamb, and pork.
- Ideal in chili, stews, and sauces
- Heat cumin and garlic in olive oil and drizzle over cooked vegetables or potatoes.

Remember: Always store herbs and spices in airtight, screw-top containers to preserve freshness.

boil, reduce heat, and simmer for 10 minutes, stirring occasionally. Set aside to cool.

4. Preheat grill to medium-high.

5. Remove the turkey steaks from marinade, discarding marinade, and grill for 4–5 minutes per side, basting with orange barbecue sauce, until the turkey steaks are fully cooked.

Diana's Grilled Rosemary Chicken

Serves 4–6
Preparation time:
 15 minutes
Grill time: 15–20 minutes

Rosemary is a wonderful aromatic spice that adds life to any dish, particularly chicken. Crushed and sprinkled at the end of grilling, the rosemary blends well with Diana Fine Herbs with Lemon Sauce. It's a simple and delicious dish.

GIVE THE MEAT A BATH
Before preparing meat, poultry, and fish for the barbecue always give it a bath. Quickly rinse the meat and pat dry before marinating or adding seasoning.

2 tbsp	25 ml	Heinz 57 BBQ Seasoning Rub (page 11)
4–6		chicken breasts, boneless and skinless
2 tbsp	25 ml	vegetable oil
¾ cup	175 ml	Diana Sauce, Fine Herbs with Lemon
1 tbsp	15 ml	chopped fresh rosemary

1. Rub chicken breasts with the Heinz 57 BBQ Seasoning Rub, pressing the seasoning into the meat. Brush chicken all over with vegetable oil. Set aside.
2. Preheat grill to medium-high.
3. Grill chicken for 5 to 6 minutes per side, basting with Diana Sauce until fully cooked and the meat is no longer pink inside.
4. Sprinkle with chopped fresh rosemary.

Grilled Seafood

Bacon-Wrapped Scallop Kebabs with Honey
   Garlic BBQ Sauce

Teriyaki Tuna with Mango Salsa

Fine Herbs with Lemon BBQ Salmon Steaks

Fine Herb with Lemon Barbecued Cedar-
   Planked Salmon

Hot and Spicy Grilled Shrimp

Foil-Pouched Sea Bass with Peaches and Chili
   Sauce

Bacon-Wrapped Scallop Kebabs with Honey Garlic BBQ Sauce

Tender and moist scallops go together with crisp and juicy bacon to create these kebabs that are suitable as an appetizer or main course. Like most seafood, scallops absorb marinades quickly. In this case, the dish is ready to grill in just an hour.

Serves 4
Marinade time: 1 hour
Preparation time:
  30 minutes
Grilling time:
  10–15 minutes

24 large		scallops (approximately 3 lbs/1.5 kg)
2 tbsp	25 ml	Heinz 57 BBQ Seasoning Rub (see page 11)
12 slices		bacon
½ cup	125 ml	Diana's Marinade, Teriyaki
½ cup	125 ml	orange juice
2 cloves		garlic, minced
1 cup	250 ml	Diana Sauce, Honey Garlic
6 skewers		8–10 inch (20–25 cm) in length

1. Soak wooden skewers in lukewarm water for at least 15 minutes.
2. Season scallops with barbecue seasoning and set aside.
3. In a large frying pan cook the bacon until slightly crisp. Remove bacon from pan and drain on paper towels. Cut each slice in half.
4. Wrap each seasoned scallop with half a slice of bacon and slide onto the skewers, ensuring the skewer holds the bacon tight. Use 6 scallops per skewer. Place scallop skewers into a glass dish.
5. Mix together the Diana's Teriyaki Marinade, orange juice, and garlic. Pour mixture over the scallop skewers, cover, and refrigerate for 1 hour.
6. Preheat grill to medium-high. Remove scallops from Diana's Marinade, discarding marinade.
7. Grill scallops for 4–5 minutes per side, basting frequently with Diana Sauce, until bacon is crisp and the scallops are just cooked. Be careful not to overcook. Serve immediately.

Nutmeg
- A pungent, sweet, and slightly bitter flavour
- Frequently used in baked goods
- Adds character to vegetables
- Excellent with potatoes, spinach, rhubarb, pears, and apples
- Essential in white sauces and cheese dishes
- Ancients used nutmeg to cure bad breath, headaches, stomach ailments, and fever
- Also used in the Middle East as an aphrodisiac

Remember: A little goes a long way, so use sparingly.

Teriyaki Tuna with Mango Salsa

Tuna steaks can be quite expensive so take great care when preparing and cooking this fish. Tuna is best grilled to rare or medium-rare. If overcooked tuna will become dry and tough. Ask your fish monger to cut your tuna steaks at least 1½ inches (3.5 cm) thick.

Serves 4
Preparation time:
  15 minutes
Grilling time: 10 minutes

2 tbsp	25 ml	cracked black peppercorns
1 tbsp	15 ml	Heinz 57 BBQ Seasoning Rub (see page 11)
1 tbsp	15 ml	sesame seeds
4 x 5 oz	150 g	tuna steaks, trimmed of skin and blood line
1 cup	250 ml	Diana's Marinade, Teriyaki
¼ cup	50 ml	honey
1		lime, juiced
2		green onions, finely chopped
1 tbsp	15 ml	chopped fresh cilantro
2 tbsp	25 ml	Heinz Tomato Ketchup
2 tbsp	25 ml	vegetable oil

Mango Salsa
Makes approximately 2 cups (500 ml)
Preparation time:
  15 minutes

SOMETHING FISHY
When grilling whole fish, use a barbecue grill basket for easy grilling and turning.

1. In a bowl combine the peppercorns, barbecue seasoning, and sesame seeds.
2. Rub the tuna steaks with the seasoning mixture, pressing it into the flesh.
3. In a bowl whisk together the Diana's Teriyaki Marinade, honey, lime juice, green onions, cilantro, and Heinz Ketchup. Set aside.
4. Preheat grill to medium-high.
5. Brush the tuna steaks with vegetable oil.
6. Grill tuna steaks for 2–3 minutes per side for rare to medium-rare, basting with the teriyaki sauce.
7. Remove from grill and slice thinly on the diagonal. Serve immediately with mango salsa.

Mango Salsa

1 ripe		mango, peeled and diced
1 small		red onion, diced
1 small		green pepper, diced
1 tbsp	15 ml	chopped fresh cilantro
1 tbsp	15 ml	Heinz Pure Apple Cider Vinegar
2 tbsp	25 ml	Heinz Ketchup Kickers, Hot and Spicy
		salt and freshly ground pepper

1. In a bowl combine the mango, red onion, green pepper, cilantro, vinegar, and Heinz Ketchup Kickers. Season to taste with salt and pepper.

Fine Herbs with Lemon BBQ Salmon Steaks

Salmon steaks are easy to prepare on the grill. Use fresh Atlantic or Pacific salmon steaks cut at least 1½-inch (3.5 cm) thick. Salmon is a healthy alternative to beef or chicken, and it contains omega-3 fatty acids, which scientists believe may play a role in helping to reduce heart disease.

Serves 6
Marinade time:
  30 minutes
Preparation time:
  15 minutes
Grilling time:
  15–20 minutes

6 x 6 oz	165 g	salmon steaks
2 tbsp	25 ml	Heinz 57 BBQ Seasoning Rub (see page 11)
1 cup	250 ml	Diana's Marinade, Lemon and Pepper
2 tbsp	25 ml	vegetable oil
1 cup	250 ml	Diana Sauce, Fine Herbs with Lemon
1		lemon, cut into 6 wedges

1. Rub the salmon steaks with the barbecue seasoning and place in a glass dish. Pour Diana's Lemon and Pepper Marinade over, turning to coat evenly. Cover and refrigerate for 30 minutes.
2. Preheat grill to medium-high.
3. Remove salmon from Diana's Marinade, discarding marinade.
4. Brush salmon steaks with oil.
5. Grill salmon steaks for 6–8 minutes per side, basting frequently with Diana Sauce until salmon is cooked and the centre bone can be pulled easily from the flesh.
6. Serve immediately with lemon wedges.

Paprika
- Part of the red pepper family
- Variety of flavours from sweet and mild to hot
- Commonly used in Hungarian cooking
- Use on scalloped potatoes, macaroni and cheese, potato salad, devilled eggs, and hors d'oeuvres for colour and flavour
- Mix with breadcrumbs before sprinkling over casseroles or vegetables

Remember: When using herbs and spices to flavour meat, rub the spices into the meat before cooking.

Fine Herb with Lemon Barbecued Cedar-Planked Salmon

This is a true Canadian grilling experience that features succulent Atlantic salmon barbecued on a cedar plank. Planking is an ancient style of cooking that traces its roots to the Haida people on Canada's West Coast. They knew that planking was the best way to cook salmon: it's fast and easy, you don't have to turn it, and the cedar adds a delicious, sweet, smoky flavour. Since it cooks quickly, the salmon doesn't dry out and by using the plank, you don't have the fuss of the fish sticking to the grill.

Serves 6
Preparation time:
  20 minutes
Grilling time:
  20–30 minutes

1		clean cedar plank (1 inch x 10 inches x 12 inches or 2.5 cm x 25 cm x 30 cm)
3		green onions, finely chopped
1 medium		red pepper, diced
1 small		red onion, finely diced
2 tbsp	25 ml	chopped fresh dill
1 tsp	5 ml	cracked black pepper
1 tbsp	15 ml	fresh lemon juice
2 tbsp	25 ml	Dijon mustard
2 tbsp	25 ml	olive oil
¾ cup	180 ml	Heinz Western Grill Mesquite BBQ Sauce
6 x 6 oz	165 g	Atlantic salmon, boneless and skinless fillets
2 tbsp	25 ml	Heinz 57 BBQ Seasoning Rub (see page 11)
		salt

THE BEST KNIVES FOR BARBECUING
Stay sharp with your barbecue by having the right knives on hand.
- *Butcher knife—light and heavy duty*
- *Filleting knife*
- *Small French knife*
- *Boning knife*
- *Paring knife*
- *Serrated knife*
- *Chef's knife*
- *Small utility knife*

1. Soak cedar plank in cold water for a minimum of 2 hours.
2. Combine green onions, red pepper, red onion, dill, black pepper, lemon juice, Dijon mustard, olive oil, and Heinz Barbecue Sauce. Season to taste with salt. Set aside.

3. Rub the barbecue seasoning onto the salmon fillets, pressing the spices into the meat. Coat each fillet with a thick layer of the vegetable mixture.
4. Preheat grill to high, about 500–600°F. Place cedar plank on grill and close barbecue lid. Heat the plank for 2–3 minutes until it begins to crackle and smoke.
5. Carefully place the salmon fillets onto the heated cedar plank. Close barbecue lid and cook the salmon for 12–15 minutes. Check the salmon every 4–5 minutes to ensure that the plank is not on fire. If necessary, use a spray bottle of water to put out the flames and reduce the heat to medium-low.
6. When the salmon is cooked, carefully remove fillets from the hot plank to a serving platter. Serve immediately.
7. Note: let cedar plank cool completely before discarding.

Hot and Spicy Grilled Shrimp

Shrimp have an amazing ability to absorb the flavours of spices and marinades very quickly. This recipe calls for a 15-minute marinade—it's ready in no time. With the help of the barbecue seasoning and Heinz Ketchup Kickers, Hot and Spicy, these shrimp burst and jump with flavour.

Serves 6
Preparation time:
 30 minutes
Grilling time:
 10–15 minutes

2 lb	900 g	jumbo shrimps (approximately 12–15 per lb)
2 tbsp	25 ml	Heinz 57 BBQ Seasoning Rub (see page 11)
6 skewers		8–10 inch (20–25 cm) in length
1 cup	250 ml	Heinz Ketchup Kickers, Hot and Spicy
1 tbsp	250 ml	Heinz Worcestershire Sauce
2 tbsp	25 ml	honey
2		green onions, finely chopped
4 cloves		garlic, finely chopped
		lemon, juiced
1 tbsp	15 ml	chopped fresh cilantro
¼ cup	50 ml	melted butter
		salt and freshly ground pepper

Separating Skewers
Always skewer meat and vegetables on separate skewers. Meat and veggies cook at different rates, so using two skewers makes it easier to time grilling.

1. Soak wooden skewers in lukewarm water for at least 15 minutes.
2. If using frozen shrimp, thaw in refrigerator overnight.
3. Shell and devein the shrimp.
4. In a large bowl toss the peeled shrimp with the barbecue seasoning, coating them completely.
5. Thread shrimp onto the metal skewers (about 5 or 6 shrimp per skewer) and place in a glass dish long enough to hold the skewered shrimp flat.
6. In a bowl mix together the Heinz Ketchup Kickers, Worcestershire sauce, honey, green onions, garlic, lemon juice, and cilantro. Season to taste with salt and pepper.

7. Pour half of this mixture over the shrimp and let marinate for at least 15 minutes.
8. Mix the remaining sauce with the melted butter.
9. Preheat grill to medium-high.
10. Grill the shrimp for 2–3 minutes per side, basting with barbecue sauce, until the shrimp are opaque and just cooked.
11. Serve immediately.

Foil-Pouched Sea Bass with Peaches and Chili Sauce

Sea bass is a delicious fish with a texture similar to salmon. It is firm and holds up well on the grill. Using sheets of tinfoil to wrap the sea bass means easy grilling and produces succulent, tender fish. In this recipe the sweetness of fresh peaches counteracts with the Chili Sauce to create a tasty combination of flavours.

Serves 4
Preparation time:
 30 minutes
Grilling time: 20 minutes

4 x 6 oz	165 g	sea bass fillets (skin and bones removed)
2 tbsp	25 ml	Heinz 57 BBQ Seasoning Rub (see page 11)
1 small		red onion, thinly sliced
1 medium		yellow pepper, thinly sliced
2 ripe		peaches, peeled, pitted, and thinly sliced
⅓ cup	100 ml	Heinz Chili Sauce, Chunky with Sweet Peppers
2 tbsp	25 ml	Heinz Pure Apple Cider Vinegar
2 tbsp	25 ml	olive oil
1 tbsp	15 ml	chopped fresh dill
		salt and freshly ground pepper
4 tbsp	50 ml	butter

First developed in 1895, Heinz Chili Sauce remains one of the most popular condiments produced by Heinz, although it contains no hot peppers! Made with tomatoes, onions, and mild spices, it adds a sweet and tangy taste to many recipes.

1. Cut 8 sheets of tin foil into 12-inch (30 cm) squares.
2. Season the sea bass fillets with the barbecue seasoning and set aside.
3. In a small bowl mix together the red onion, pepper, peaches, Heinz Chili Sauce, vinegar, olive oil, and dill. Season to taste with salt and pepper.
4. Place two sheets of tin foil one on top of the other.
5. Divide peach mixture onto 8. Place one-eighth of peach mixture in the centre of the tin foil. Place one seasoned sea bass fillet on top of the peach mixture. Top with another eighth of the peach mixture. Top with 1 tbsp (15 ml) of butter.

6. Starting from the bottom fold the tinfoil over the sea bass. Fold in both sides and then roll up to enclose the fillet. Press firmly to secure the bundle. Repeat with remaining sea bass fillets.
7. These bundles can be made up to 2 hours ahead and refrigerated.
8. Preheat the grill to medium-high.
9. Place bundles on the grill and cook for 6–8 minutes per side, turning once.
10. Remove from grill, gently unwrap each bundle, and serve with fresh orange slices.

Side Dishes

Grilled Jumbo Mushrooms

Diana's Original Grill Roasted Potatoes

Grilled Zucchini Provençal

BBQ Baked Beans

Super-Smashed Potatoes

Grilled Jumbo Mushrooms

Serves 6
Preparation time:
  15 minutes
Grilling time: 15 minutes

HERB SPREADS
To enjoy the tast of fresh herbs, chop them up and mix with soft-ened butter. Herb butter tastes great on vegetables and fish.

Grilling mushrooms on the barbecue enhances their deli-cate taste. The addition of Diana Sauce to this slightly spicy marinade introduces a new flavour to this wonderful side dish.

12		jumbo white mushrooms
2 cups	500 ml	Diana Sauce, Cracked Pepper
1 cup	250 ml	soy sauce
1 cup	250 ml	balsamic vinegar
¼ cup	50 ml	chopped fresh cilantro
2 tsp	10 ml	crushed red chilies
2 tsp	10 ml	sesame oil

1. Mix together Diana Sauce, soy sauce, balsamic vinegar, cilantro, chilies, and sesame oil and pour over the mushrooms, ensuring they are completely covered with marinade, then refrigerate for 2–4 hours.
2. Preheat grill to high.
3. Drain the mushrooms and transfer to a grill basket.
4. Grill for 4–5 minutes per side.
5. Carefully remove the cooked mushrooms from the grill and serve.
6. Garnish with fresh cilantro.

Diana's Original Grill Roasted Potatoes

There's nothing better than the taste of grilled potatoes—crisp on the outside – tender on the inside. With a sprinkle of basil and a dash of oregano, these spuds make an excellent side dish to any main course.

Serves 4 to 6
Preparation time:
  30 minutes
Grill time: 15–20 minutes

2 lbs	900 g	red potatoes, washed and cut in quarters
3 tbsp	45 ml	vegetable oil
1 tsp	5 ml	dried basil and oregano
1 tsp	5 ml	salt
¼ tsp	1 ml	pepper
¾ cup	175 ml	Diana Sauce, Original

1. Place potatoes in a large pot and cover with cold water. Bring potatoes to a rolling boil, reduce heat to low, and simmer for 5 minutes. Drain potatoes and place evenly onto a baking sheet, allowing the potatoes to cool slightly.
2. Season potatoes with oil, basil, oregano, salt, and pepper.
3. Preheat grill to medium-high.
4. Place potato wedges in a vegetable grilling basket and grill for 6 to 8 minutes per side, turning every few minutes and basting with the Diana Sauce until they are lightly charred, fully cooked, tender and crisp.
5. Carefully remove potatoes from the grilling basket and serve immediately.
6. Note: if you do not have a grilling basket use a perforated pizza pan on the grill instead.
7. Garnish with fresh parsley, if desired.

Basil
- A sweet, herbal bouquet
- Ideal match for tomato-based sauces, pizza, and tomatoes
- Toss with green and yellow beans, grilled peppers, and eggplant
- Adds a minty aroma when crumbled or chopped over grilled or baked chicken, lamb, and fish
- Whisk into vinaigrettes and quiches
- Blends well with garlic, thyme, and oregano

Remember: All dried spices should be stored in cool, dark, dry places.

Grilled Zucchini Provençal

Serves 6–8
Marinade time: 1 hour
Preparation time:
 10 minutes
Grilling time: 15 minutes

Set sail for the tastes of Provence with these colourfully delicious boats carved from zucchini. The cargo on these vessels is a combination of cheese, garlic, leeks, and onions in a mixture of one of Heinz's Ketchup Kickers and a Diana's Marinade.

4 medium		zucchini
½ cup	125 ml	Diana's Marinade, Garlic and Herbs
2 tbsp	25 ml	oil
2 small		onions, diced
2		leeks, diced
1		red pepper, seeded and diced
2 tbsp	25 ml	garlic, minced
¼ cup	50 ml	Heinz Chili Sauce, Chunky with Sweet Peppers
¼ cup	50 ml	Heinz Ketchup Kickers, Sweet Basil and Oregano
1 cup	250 ml	parmesan cheese, grated

GET THE BASKET
When grilling vegetables on the barbecue, use a specially designed grilling basket, which can be found in most hardware stores. A grilling basket takes the frustration out of cooking vegetables by allowing you to turn many vegetables at once, and results in a more even and faster method of cooking.

1. Preheat grill to medium-high.
2. Cut zucchini in half lengthwise and carefully scoop the seeds out of the centre with a spoon, creating a boat.
3. Cover with Diana's Garlic and Herbs Marinade and let stand for 1 hour.
3. Heat oil in a medium-sized non-stick pan.
4. Over medium heat sauté onions, leeks, peppers, and garlic until soft but not browned.
5. Remove from heat and stir in Heinz Chili Sauce and Heinz Ketchup Kickers.
6. Preheat grill to medium-high.
7. Remove zucchini from Diana's Marinade, discarding marinade.
8. Spoon onion-tomato mixture into zucchini boats and top with parmesan cheese.
9. Grill covered for 12–15 minutes or until zucchini is cooked, the stuffing is heated, and the cheese has browned.

BBQ
Baked Beans

With barbecue cooking there really are no rules anymore. Baked beans are most often associated with breakfast and campfire cooking, but they make an excellent side dish when cooked on the grill.

Serves 8
Preparation time:
  10 minutes
Cooking time: 45 minutes

2 x 14 oz cans	398 ml	Heinz Original Baked Beans in Tomato Sauce
1 medium		onion, diced
4 cloves		garlic, minced
8 slices		bacon, fully cooked and coarsely chopped
½ cup	125 ml	maple syrup
¼ cup	50 ml	Heinz Ketchup Kickers, Hot and Spicy
2 tsp	10 ml	Heinz Worcestershire sauce
¼ cup	50 ml	Heinz Western Grill Garlic BBQ Sauce
		salt and freshly ground pepper

1. Preheat oven to 350°F (180°C).
2. In a large ovenproof dish combine the Heinz Beans, onion, garlic, bacon, maple syrup, Heinz Ketchup Kickers, Worcestershire sauce, and barbecue sauce. Season to taste with salt and pepper.
3. Cover and bake for 45 minutes. Stir and serve.

Super-Smashed Potatoes

Serves 4
Preparation time:
  45 minutes

What's the difference between mashed potatoes and smashed potatoes? With smashed potatoes you keep a few lumps in the potatoes to make it more interesting to eat.

5 large		**Yukon gold potatoes, peeled and quartered**
1 cup	**250 ml**	**Heinz Western Grill Garlic BBQ Sauce**
2 medium		**onions, peeled and cut into ½-inch (1 cm) rounds**
2 cups	**500 ml**	**cheddar, grated**
¼ cup	**50 ml**	**cream**
		salt and freshly ground pepper

THE WRAP ON POTATOES
When you cook potatoes wrapped in aluminum foil be sure to serve them hot or refrigerate them immediately after cooking. The foil can trap moisture that can encourage the growth of bacteria and botulism.

1. Preheat grill to medium.
2. Toss onion rounds in the barbecue sauce and grill for 10–12 minutes or until the onions are lightly charred and softened. Cool, coarsely chop, and set aside.
3. Place potatoes in a small pot and cover with lightly salted water. Bring to a boil and let simmer until the potatoes are fully cooked. Drain potatoes and return to the pot.
4. Add cheese, cream, and onions and smash well. Season with salt and pepper to taste and serve immediately.

Desserts

Spiced Double Chewy Chocolate Chip Cookies

Heinz Apple Pie

Spiced Double Chewy Chocolate Chip Cookies

This may be called a cookie recipe but it could be confused for a mini-muffin. It's a chocolate chip explosion made with Heinz Ketchup! If you're a cookie monster, try doubling or tripling the recipe, and freezing the left over raw cookie dough for future use.

Makes approximately 24 cookies
Preparation time: 30 minutes
Cooking time: 8–12 minutes

6 oz	165 ml	bittersweet chocolate
6 tbsp	90 ml	butter, room temperature
½ cup	125 ml	brown sugar, lightly packed
¼ cup	50 ml	Heinz Tomato Ketchup
1 large		egg
1 tsp	5 ml	vanilla
½ tsp	1 ml	cinnamon
1 pinch		salt
⅔ cup + 2 tbsp	180 g + 25 g	all purpose flour, sifted
¼ cup	50 ml	cocoa powder, sifted
1 cup	250 ml	chocolate chips

1. Preheat oven to 350° F (180° C).
2. Melt chocolate over a double boiler or in a microwave.
3. Mix butter, sugar, Heinz Ketchup, egg, vanilla, cinnamon, and salt with a hand mixer or wooden spoon until smooth.
4. Add the melted chocolate and mix on low until incorporated.
5. Add flour and cocoa and mix on low until incorporated.
6. Fold in the chips and drop teaspoon-size potions onto a greased or parchment lined cookie sheet.
7. Bake for 8–12 minutes until an inserted toothpick is pulled out clean.

Heinz
Apple Pie

Serves 8
Preparation time:
 1½ hours
Cooking time: 45 minutes

Cinnamon

- A sweet, woody fragrance
- Cinnamon was the motivation for world exploration in the 15th and 16th centuries
- Cinnamon sticks are long pieces of bark from an evergreen tree that are rolled, pressed, and dried
- Most common baking spice; used in cakes, cookies, and desserts throughout the world
- Also used in savoury chicken and lamb dishes from the Middle East
- Often paired with apples and used in other fruit and cereal dishes
- Stick cinnamon is used in pickling and for flavouring hot beverages

Remember: In casseroles and stews add whole spices at start of cooking.

Here is a recipe for those who need to have ketchup with every thing.

1½ cups	350 g	all purpose flour
⅓ cup	100 g	sugar
⅔ cup	180 g	cold butter, cut in small cubes
1		egg
1 tsp	25 ml	salt
1 tsp	5 ml	cinnamon
1 tbsp	15 ml	water, ice cold
2½ lbs	1 kg	cooking apples, peeled, cored and cut in small chunks
¼ cup	50 ml	Heinz Tomato Ketchup
¼ cup	50 ml	rum soaked raisins (optional)
3 tbsp	45 g	brown sugar
2 tbsp	25 ml	lemon juice

1. For the dough, mix flour, sugar, butter, salt, egg, water, and cinnamon until fully incorporated and rest for 1 hour in the fridge.
2. Roll the dough to about ⅜ of an inch and cut in half, one to fit into an 8-inch pie dish and one for the top.
3. Lightly grease your pie tin or dish and press the dough gently but firmly into place.
4. Toss together the apples, Heinz Ketchup, raisins, brown sugar, and lemon juice and fill the pie shell.
5. Place the top on the pie and press around the edges to create a seal. Cut away excess dough.
6. Bake for 45 minutes at 350° F (180° C).

Index